Caroline Walsh

# "The Homes of Irish Writers"

ANVIL BOOKS

First published 1982
by Anvil Books Limited
90 Lower Baggot Street, Dublin 2

Text © Caroline Walsh 1982

ISBN 0 900068 54 X case
ISBN 0 900068 71 X paper

*Typesetting Computertype Limited*
*Printed in the Republic of Ireland*
*by Cahill Printers Limited*

*Frontispiece*
*Bust of William Butler Yeats*
*outside Sandymount Castle, Dublin*

For my mother,
Mary Lavin,
and my stepfather,
Michael McDonald Scott

# *Special Acknowledgments*

I would like specially to thank The Irish Times
newspaper where I work as a reporter and feature
writer, and where the articles from which this book
grew were originally printed.

To thank Fergus Pyle, then the paper's editor,
who first suggested that I write a regular column,
and the late, dear, Donal Foley who gave endless
encouragement with the project.

To thank the Arts and Studies department, the
Library, especially John Gibson and Tony Lennon,
and the Photographic department.

Thanks also to the National Library, Bord Fáilte,
Maurice Craig, Michael Minihane and Colin
Smythe for invaluable help in supplying photo-
graphs.

# Contents

# Introduction

The relationship between Ireland and its most famous writers is beset by the curious phenomenon that though many of them eventually left it to make their lives elsewhere, few could ever forget it. For instance, though the playwright Sir Richard Steele (1672–1729), who was born in Bull Alley in Dublin, left the country at the age of thirteen he was nevertheless described years later by Thackeray as undoubtedly an Irishman, and the same can be said about Richard Brinsley Sheridan (1751–1816). Born at 12 Upper Dorset Street, Dublin, and educated at Samuel Whyte's school in Grafton Street, now Bewley's Cafe, he left Ireland at the age of eight, yet one of his last utterances in the House of Commons was a plea for his homeland. 'If they were to be the last words I should ever utter in this house,' he told his colleagues prophetically, 'I should say, "Be just to Ireland, as you value your own honour; be just to Ireland, as you value your own peace." '

This book, therefore, is about the Ireland that its writers knew. It is not about the imagined houses of their books but about the houses in which they themselves were either born or lived, or died if they had not already emigrated. It is not a book about the many English authors who visited Ireland like Scott or Shelley, Thackeray or Trollope, nor is it about the many eminent writers in the Irish language like Tomas O Criomhthain, Peig Sayers and Muiris O Suilleabhain, that trinity that gave literary immortality to the Blasket islands off the Kerry coast. Theirs is another story and must be left to the person who can tell it in the language in which they themselves wrote. Neither is it about the host of Irish patriot writers – Thomas Davis, John Mitchel, Padraic Pearse, Thomas MacDonagh, Joseph Mary Plunkett and many

others– for theirs too is a separate story.

My guiding principle was to include writers whose homes meant something special to them; ideally those whose homes are still standing today, even if in ruins. Inevitably many writers had to be omitted from the main text but the purpose of this introduction is to mention some of them, beginning in the seventeenth century when in addition to Steele there were three other Restoration dramatists with Irish connections. Though Thomas Southerne (1660–1746) spent the best part of his life in London, he was born in the Oxmanstown Road area of Dublin and educated at Trinity, the college from which George Farquhar (1678–1707), born in Shipquay Street, Derry, had the dubious distinction of being expelled – for telling a profane joke, or so it was said. Their colleague William Congreve (1670–1729), although born in England, came to Ireland as a child when his father was stationed at an army garrison, first in Youghal, County Cork, and later in Carrickfergus, County Antrim. While in Ireland, both Farquhar and Congreve attended the illustrious Kilkenny College, a college whose most famous pupil was Jonathan Swift.

The life of Swift is, according to one critic, a heavily mined area and certainly, though over three hundred years have passed since his birth, no one is yet possessed of the full facts of his life. Accordingly, though his birth is commemorated in Dublin by a plaque on a wall in Ship Street just outside the lower yard of Dublin Castle, the message it contains is a qualified one: 'In 7 Hoey's Court (now demolished) about 100 ft. north west of this spot it is *reputed* that Jonathan Swift, Dean of St. Patrick's Cathedral was born on 30th day of Nov. 1667. He died on

*St. Patrick's Cathedral,
Dublin (left)
Goldsmith's statue outside
Trinity College, Dublin
(right)*

the 19th day of Oct. 1745.' Having passed through Trinity College and taken holy orders he got the living of Kilroot, County Antrim, where he took up residence on the shores of Belfast Lough. Later he became vicar at Laracor, County Meath, where a tablet now commemorates that period of his life: 'Church of Ireland. Church of St. Peter. Laracor. This is the site of the parish church of which Jonathan Swift was vicar'.

Further along the road, on the way to Trim, are the remains of a cottage where Esther Johnson, to whom he addressed *The Journal to Stella.* was said to have lived. Although Esther Vanhomrigh, the subject of his poem *Cadenus and Vanessa*, loved Swift and pined for him at her home in County Kildare, Marley Abbey, now called Celbridge Abbey, it is beside Stella that he is buried in St. Patrick's Cathedral. Here on the wall his epitaph is written in Latin. Translated many times it can be rendered: 'Here lies the body of Jonathan Swift S.T.D., Dean of this Cathedral, where savage indignation can no longer lacerate his heart. Go, traveller, and emulate, if you can, the heroic exertions of this champion of liberty.'

There is also doubt about the birthplace of Oliver Goldsmith, born circa 1728 who died in 1774, and of whom a leader writer in *The Irish Times* once wrote in exasperation: 'Where he was born remains, like the identity of St. Patrick, the source of perennial dispute. But it was somewhere in Ireland and he belongs to this nation.' Though some believe that he was born at his grandmother's home near Elphin, County Roscommon, others give the location of his birth as Pallas, near Ballymahon, County Longford, where his father, a clergyman, farmed and assisted at such nearby churches as that at Forgney. When he was appointed to the parish of Kilkenny West in nearby County Westmeath, the family moved to Lissoy, regarded by many as the Auburn of his poem *The Deserted Village*. It was in Lissoy that Oliver contracted the smallpox which left him scarred all his life; here too he received his early education, later progressing to schools in Elphin, Athlone, and Edgeworthstown. At Trinity he paid his way by acting as a sizar whose duties included waiting on tables and sweeping out courtyards. Ultimately, disillusioned at his inability to settle to a career, the family packed him off to England where to their surprise he was to make his name.

Laurence Sterne (1713–1768), author of *Tristram Shandy*, was born in Clonmel, County Tipperary, when his father, an army subaltern, was temporarily stationed in the town. The writer is, however, much more associated with the little village of Annamoe in County Wicklow where as a child, while staying with relatives at the local parsonage, he fell into the mill race while the mill was working; he was rescued unhurt to the astonishment of the locals.

Thomas Moore (1779–1852), who today is far better remembered for his songs than for *Lalla Rookh*, the long poem it took him four years to write, was born at 12 Aungier Street in Dublin where his father had a grocery store. Though a pub now stands on the site of the house, it bears the writer's name and proclaims him in a plaque to be 'Ireland's lyric poet'. Here, at the musical evenings given regularly by his mother, young Moore would sing popular songs of the day especially those by the composer Dibdin, author of *Tom Bowling*. After he grew famous in England, he still visited home and was one of the many eminent men of his day who gathered at the soirées given in Dublin by the novelist Lady Morgan (c. 1783–1859).

Though more eminent nineteenth-century novelists are included in this book, none surely can have been gayer or more outgoing than Lady Morgan, born Miss Sydney Owenson, who first achieved fame through her book *The Wild Irish Girl*, much of which she wrote at Longford House, Beltra, County Sligo, home of the Crofton family to which she was related. Though her birthplace is uncertain, it was either in Dublin or on board a ship travelling towards it across the Irish sea that she first saw the light of day; her mother, a young Englishwoman, was coming to join her actor husband in Ireland.

As a young woman, the future novelist worked first as a governess, then as a companion, to three distinguished Irish families, starting with the Featherstonhaughs who lived at Bracklyn Castle, Killucan, County Westmeath; here, though she was the life and soul of the family, entertaining them with songs and jigs, she was even then rising early in the morning to work on her writings. After a while with the Crawford family at Fort William in County Tipperary, she went to the Abercorn family at their imposing seat, Barons Court, Newtown-stewart, County Tyrone. It was through them that she met Charles Morgan, the young English doctor she eventually married in spite of 'the dreadful certainty of being parted forever from a country and friends I love' which made her hesitate initially. As things turned out, however, they lived many years of their life together in Dublin, at 35 Kildare Street, a street which though it houses such prestigious institutions as the Parliament, the National Museum and the National Library, is today filled mostly with office blocks. The number of her house there was years later changed to No. 39. Here with her husband, who early on received a title, she gave lavish soirées and musical evenings to the strains of the piano, the harp and the Spanish guitar. Looking in later years through her visiting book, she recalled that in its heyday 'representatives of the four quarters of the earth had passed through my little taudis in Kildare Street'. When Paganini came she organized a dinner in the Florentine style for his benefit to which he responded with such plaudits as *bravissimo* and *excellentissimo*. And once, eager to get up a party in haste for Thomas Moore, she issued invitations by throwing open her windows and asking her friends as they passed, in their carriages and cabs, in the street below. When Lord Melbourne granted her a pension of £300 a year, the Morgans left Ireland and though she claimed it had often slighted and persecuted her, she was still lonely to be going. Nor did she forget Ireland when living permanently in England. Shortly before her death she gave a lively party on St. Patrick's Day, while in her will, among other provisions, she left £100 for the erection of a marble tablet in St. Patrick's Cathedral, honouring O Carolan, the blind harpist.

Among the young men who had come to Lady Morgan's salon in Dublin was Samuel Lover (1797–1868), author of such novels as *Rory O'More* and *Handy Andy,* one of whose own Dublin addresses was 9 d'Olier Street. Having left Ireland in the 1830s he capitalized on his nationality by devising a show called his *Irish Entertainment* which he put on in England and America and which consisted of imitations of the Irish peasantry and renditions of his own songs and poems.

Not all the novelists of this period, however, were part of Dublin society, and one of the exceptions was Gerald Griffin (1803–1840), author of *The Collegians*. Born in Bow Lane, Limerick, he was reared in Brunswick Street , later renamed Sarsfield Street, and outside the town at Carrowbane, near Loughill, in a house called Fairy Lawn. When his parents emigrated to Pennsylvania, he moved with some brothers and sisters to the vicinity of nearby Adare, and though he never saw his father or mother again it was to them he sent the entire £800 he made from *The Collegians*. The murder trial on which the novel was based also inspired Benedict's opera *The Lily of Killarney*. Griffin also lived in Pallaskenry, in County Limerick. Though as a young man he did fall in love, it was with a married woman, Lydia Fisher, and shortly afterwards he retired from secular life to become a Christian Brother, first at North Richmond Street in Dublin, later transferring to the North Monastery in Cork where he died of typhus and was buried in the community cemetery.

In Dublin, meanwhile, the genre of the Gothic novel had been developed by the Reverend Charles Robert Maturin (1782–1824), most famous for his novel *Melmoth the Wanderer*. Though early in his career he worked for a short time as a curate in Loughrea, County Galway, most of his life was spent in charge of St. Peter's, Aungier Street, Dublin. Conveniently he lived just around the corner at 37 York Street which, though now long gone, was a lively place in Maturin's time. According to one contemporary account, the walls of its parlours were once painted with scenes from his novels, the ceilings decorated like cloud-filled skies dotted here and there with eagles. So fond was he of dancing that he would occasionally draw the curtains across in the morning to keep the light out and give quadrille parties as if it were night. An eccentric, he was once spotted dashing through the streets, a shoe on one foot, a boot on the other, while another quirk was to paste a wafer on his forehead when he felt literary inspiration coming on, to alert the family that he should be left in peace. Most of his writing was done either at York Street or in Marsh's Library, but financial difficulties made his life very hard, probably in the end hastening his death.

The Gothic tradition was continued in Ireland by Joseph Sheridan

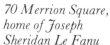

*70 Merrion Square,*
*home of Joseph*
*Sheridan Le Fanu*

Le Fanu (1814–1873), novelist and short story writer, famous for such works as *Shamus O'Brien, Uncle Silas* and *The House by the Churchyard*. Though some say he was born at 45 Lower Dominick Street, Dublin, his birthplace is usually recorded as The Royal Hibernian Military School (now St. Mary's Hospital) in the Phoenix Park, where his father was chaplin. It was certainly there that he spent his early years until his father was appointed Dean of Emly, when they moved to the rectory at Abington just outside Limerick city. Here, apart from bird nesting and nutting in the woods, one of the chief thrills of young Le Fanu's childhood was to travel aboard the steamship *Garry Owen* to the seaside resort of Kilkee for the day. As an adult he lived in a number of Dublin houses including 2 Nelson Street, 1 and later 15 Warrington Place, and finally 70 (then 15) Merrion Square, now the headquarters of the Arts Council. Here he became almost as odd as the characters in his books, gradually withdrawing from the world to such an extent that the people of Dublin called him the invisible prince. Writing in bed by the light of two candles from midnight to dawn, when he did sleep he was tormented with nightmares which, as the doctor treating him said, seemed in the end to almost overpower him. He is buried in Mount Jerome cemetery.

Without a doubt his successor in the Irish Gothic tradition was Bram Stoker (1847–1912), author of *Dracula*, who, before he went to England to be the manager of the actor Henry Irving, lived at 15 Marino Crescent, Clontarf, Dublin.

The macabre strain was not, however, confined to fiction. It runs too through the poetry of James Clarence Mangan (1803–1849) who at

15

*Fishamble Street, Dublin, in
1797 (left)
Curragh Chase, near Adare,
County Limerick (right)*

one point either lived or worked at 6 York Street, now demolished,
near the home of Maturin who was his hero. Born at 3 Fishamble
Street, also now long gone, his childhood was poor and unhappy and
he grew up into a sinister individual, easily spotted in the city because
of the odd garb he wore, which included a wig, giant green spectacles,
and voluminous umbrellas usually carried one on either arm. His end
was as hard as his beginning. Having taken ill in his cheap lodgings in
Bride Street, either from malnutrition or cholera which was then ram-
pant in the city, he was admitted to the Meath Hospital where he died.
He was buried in Glasnevin cemetery.

Sir Samuel Ferguson (1810–1886), according to Yeats the most Irish
of Irish poets, was born at 23 High Street, Belfast. Taking up the story
from there he says, 'During my childhood the family resided at Cider
Court, near Crumlin, and afterwards at The Throne, near Belfast, and
Collon in Glenwhirry, where I received those impressions of nature
and romance which have more or less influenced all my habits of
thought and sentiment in after life.' He also holidayed with cousins at
a place called Tildarg where, as he afterwards recalled, they used to
lean over a bridge, throwing bluebells into the Drumadarragh river.
After making his life in Dublin where he married one of the Guinness
family, his home at 20 North Great George's Street earned the
nickname, The Ferguson Arms, because of his great propensity for
entertaining. Recalling the dances, musical evenings, conversaziones,
and Shakespearian evenings that he organized there, his widow and
biographer, Lady Ferguson, later wrote that one of his chief priorities
in life was to make his friends feel welcome at his home. After his death

16

at Strand Lodge, a friend's house in the seaside resort of Howth just outside Dublin, his body was taken to Donegore, County Antrim, for burial with his ancestors.

The poet Aubrey de Vere (1814–1902), son of a Protestant landed family in County Limerick, was born at Curragh Chase, the de Vere's ancestral home near Adare. Because of the family's long association with the place it was for him, he once wrote, haunted ground. There, 'the past becomes so distinct that I recognize the steps of the departed as well as their voices. The most trivial incidents rise up before me wherever I go; and in every room of the house and every walk of the garden or woods I see again the old gestures, expressions of face, even accidents of dress which no one could fancy could have lived in the memory . . . .' On a hill close to the house he lit a bonfire as a boy to celebrate the passing of the Catholic Emancipation Bill, and later he renounced the faith of his fathers and became a Catholic. During the famine when 'in the course of one month we saw nearly the whole food of the great mass of the country melt like snow before our eyes,' he threw himself into working for the relief of the people he saw suffering on all sides. When he died at Curragh Chase it was in the same small room looking out over the deer-park that he had occupied as a boy, and, though the funeral took place when the roads were almost impassable with snow and hail, representatives of such prominent southern families as the Dunravens, Inchiquins and Monteagles came to follow him to his last resting-place in the Protestant cemetery at nearby Askeaton. Curragh Chase was gutted by fire in 1941.

The poet William Allingham (1824–1889) was also rooted in the

17

place where he was born, Ballyshannon, County Donegal. 'The little town where I was born has a voice of its own, low, solemn, persistent, humming through the air day and night, summer and winter,' he once wrote, the voice being that of the river Erne to which he gave literary immortality in his poems. Born, as he tells us, in a street running down into the harbour, the family had several homes in the town in his youth, but the house he liked best was called The Cottage; covered in clematis and japonica it also had a walnut tree in the garden. Though his work as a customs official took him to other towns in the north of Ireland and finally to Lymington in England, when he died his ashes were brought home for burial in Ballyshannon.

Another writer of the nineteenth century was Dion Boucicault (c. 1820–1890) who, though he wrote, adapted or doctored over two hundred plays, is remembered chiefly for *Arrah-na-Pogue, Conn the Shaughraun* and *The Colleen Bawn* which he adapted from *The Collegians.* Doubts hover not only over his date and place of birth but also over his parentage. However it is generally believed that he was the illegitimate son of Mrs. Anne Boursiquot, wife of a Dublin wine merchant of Huguenot extraction, and Dr. Dionysius Lardner, a lecturer at Trinity, who lodged in her home. Dion is said to have been born at 28 Middle Gardiner Street in Dublin, the family later moving to No. 47 on the lower end of the same street. When he emigrated to England his brogue got him such Irish parts on the stage as that of the title role in an adaptation of *Rory O'More* and certainly he never forgot his native land. When asked on one occasion if he was Irish he replied, 'Sir, nature did me that honour.' When many years later he came back to Dublin to star in his plays he was entertained by such doyens of society as Lady Ferguson and Lady Wilde, and followed through the streets by the general public like the true prodigal son.

When the Celtic Revival took place, giving birth to the Abbey Theatre, other playwrights emerged. One of these was Lady Gregory's neighbour, Edward Martyn (1859–1923), the wealthy son of a Catholic landowning family whose seat was Tulira Castle near Ardrahan, County Galway. An old tower house, it was updated and added to during Martyn's time, much to the distaste of W. B. Yeats, but Martyn himself led a life of great simplicity there, spending much of his time in a sparsely furnished bedroom and study in the old tower block. Occasionally after dinner he would play his organ in the Gothic

*Tulira Castle, County Galway, home of Edward Martyn*

hallway of the house. The author of such plays as *The Heather Field* and *Maeve,* he was dominated for most of his life by his mother and never married. When he died, his body, by his own request, was given up for dissection by medical students and subsequently buried in a pauper's grave. In his will he bequeathed his library to the Carmelite order.

George Fitzmaurice (1877–1963), author of *The Country Dressmaker* and *The Pie Dish,* was another contemporary playwright and had his roots in County Kerry. The son of a Protestant clergyman, his home was Bedford House near Listowel, though most of his life was spent in Dublin where he died in a rented room in No. 3 Harcourt Street and was buried in Mount Jerome cemetery.

The poet and playwright Padraic Colum (1881–1972) was born in Longford town, where his father was Master of the workhouse. There as a child he got used to the whispered talk of the paupers as they shuffled through the wards. But the place had a bright side too, the garden where he would traipse along after his mother learning the magical names of the plants that grew there, pinks and peonies, hollyhock and London pride. When his father became a stationmaster in Dublin they moved to a cottage beside the rail station at Eden Road, Glasthule, where Padraic was within easy reach of the seaside town of Kingstown, now Dun Laoghaire. Here he often rooted in the stalls outside the local shops for the penny dreadfuls he adored, and watched, mesmerized, the beautiful people who came to the yacht clubs on the waterfront, attended garden-parties at the elegant terraced houses or sauntered leisurely up and down the pier. Though he later emigrated to America he came home regularly to stay with his sister in the Ranelagh area of Dublin at 11 Edenvale Road. When he died he was brought home to be buried with his wife, Mary, by the sea in St. Fintan's cemetery, Sutton, County Dublin.

James Stephens (1880–1950), author of *The Crock of Gold* and *The Charwoman's Daughter,* was born in the heart of Dublin, in the shadow of St. Catherine's Church, at 5 Thomas Court off Thomas Street. At their next home, 5 Artigan's Dwellings off Buckingham Street, his father died and subsequently they moved to 8 St. Joseph's Road, off Prussia Street, where they were living when he was picked up for begging or wandering alone in the streets and committed to the Meath Protestant Industrial School for Boys on Carysfort Avenue, Blackrock. Possibly this was the making of him as here he got a fine education. As an adult, his last home in Ireland was a flat on the top floor of 42 Fitzwilliam Place, within easy reach of the National Gallery on Merrion Square where for a time he worked as Registrar. In 1925 he went to live permanently in London, only returning to Ireland on occasional visits.

As one comes closer to the present day so many names come to mind that it is not possible to include them all. Among those from the north of Ireland, there is novelist Forrest Reid (1875–1947), a native of the city of Belfast, who lived at 13 Ormiston Crescent from the 1920s on; C. S. Lewis (1898–1963), born at 47 Dundela Avenue, who described his Belfast childhood in his autobiography *Surprised by Joy;* the poet Louis MacNeice (1907–1963), also born in Belfast, who spent his childhood at his father's rectory in Carrickfergus as he relates in his unfinished autobiography, *The Strings are False;* and Flann O'Brien (1911–1966) author of *At-Swim-Two-Birds,* of Strabane, County Tyrone, who lived most of his life in Dublin.

From the far south comes Daniel Corkery (1878–1964) who at one of his Cork homes, 1 Auburn Villas, Gardiners Hill, entertained such young authors as the short story writer Frank O'Connor (1903–1966), himself born in Cork in Douglas Street and reared at 251 Blarney Lane and in a house in Harrington Square.

Lennox Robinson (1886–1958), dramatist and stalwart of the Abbey Theatre for so many years, was born in County Cork in a house called Westgrove on Donnybrook Hill in Douglas, just outside Cork city. Here, as a child, he revelled in the parties given by his parents at which bands from the local barracks played, and where dance cards, accompanied by little pink, white and blue pencils ordered specially for the

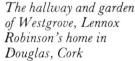
*The hallway and garden of Westgrove, Lennox Robinson's home in Douglas, Cork*

occasion, were given out. So sad was Lennox, then called Stuart, when it came to leaving Westgrove that he threw his arms out wide to embrace and kiss the old laburnum tree. 'Good-bye Galtees and tennis court, grass garden and fruit garden and beloved laburnum. Never, never again. Good-bye!' he later wrote in the evocative memoir he wrote with his sister Nora and brother Tom, which they called *Three Homes*. Looking back in 1938 he added: 'For all us children something had gathered round Westgrove, some sentiment so precious, so almost sacred, that not a single child has ventured to visit it in more than forty years.'

Their next County Cork home was 5 Fisher Street, Kinsale. They were fascinated by the Inniskilling Fusiliers who were quartered there, especially when on Sundays, wearing their great busbys, they marched through town to church accompanied by a band. Later their youthful interest in those soldiers was heightened by the tragedy that soon befell many of them: 'They marched off one morning to the South African war and we never saw them again.' Stuart had gone with his father to the quays to see them off and within a few weeks news of the Tugela and of Spion Kop began to come in. Each afternoon he would be dispatched for a copy of *The Irish Times* so that the family could keep up with all this news.

Their next home was at Ballymoney near Ballineen, also in County Cork, where their father was rector, and from here Nora left the family to be married and make a life in India. So heartbroken was Stuart that never afterwards could he stand on the platform of Cork station without remembering how desolate he had felt as a boy when she

21

*Boru House,*
*Mulgrave Street,*
*Limerick, home of*
*Kate O'Brien*

disappeared down its tunnel, going out of his life for so many years.

Later, Lennox left to make his life in Dublin, where the house most associated with him is Sorrento in Dalkey, a suburb of Dublin, where the garden sloped down to the sea and looked out over Killiney Bay to Bray Head and the Wicklow Hills. Here, plays were staged in the grounds. Here, too, Robinson's mother, who had come to live with him, died: 'On a still April evening, the garden gay with the spring flowers she loved and the blackbirds and thrushes singing their maddest, her last words to us were "Good night, dear children." '

Country names include Brinsley MacNamara (1890–1963) of Delvin, County Westmeath, famous for his novel *The Valley of the Squinting Windows*, and F. R. Higgins (1897–1941), the poet from Foxford, County Mayo, who immortalized County Meath in his poems and who is buried today in the grounds of what was once Swift's church at Laracor.

In Limerick the great writer of the twentieth century was Kate O'Brien (1897–1974) who grew up in Boru House, a solid redbrick dwelling in Mulgrave Street. As her mother died when she was a small girl, however, she spent most of her free time at the Presentation Convent in Sexton Street where her two aunts, Mary and Fan, were nuns. Remembering it she wrote: 'We children on feast days or special days were permitted to stay long hours "in the parlour" with our aunts. We loved to do so, because we were spoiled there, running wild in the kitchen garden and among the lovely chicken runs, allowed to play the piano, and sometimes to examine the sacristy – and stuffed all the time with refreshments – puff cracknels, Madeira cake, milk and pears and all delights.' On Christmas Day between noon and 3 pm the whole family would assemble in that parlour with its highly polished floor, its Victorian chairs, its plants in brass pots, its two portraits of bishops on the wall, and its piano, to the accompaniment of which Kate's sisters would sing *The Battle Eve of the Irish Brigade* and *The Snowy Breasted Pearl*. While the adults drank port and ate Turkish Delight, Kate's father would entertain them by juggling oranges and apples.

Kate herself attended Laurel Hill school, the convent run by the Faithful Companions of Jesus. It was an experience that she was to draw on heavily when she wrote *The Land of Spices. Without my Cloak*, the book that won her the Hawthornden prize in England, was just one of the novels she set in the Limerick area which she loved greatly and to which she dedicated her book *My Ireland*: 'With warmest love as my father Tom O'Brien would have thought proper, I humbly dedicate this little book to Limerick, my dear native place.' She especially loved Sarsfield bridge: 'I always like to go slowly either way, across this bridge, for from it there is everything to see – all of life and one's own regrets and sentimentalities.'

Later she had a home in Roundstone, County Galway, which the locals believed was haunted: 'In Roundstone there were many legends about my house, and many long acquainted with the village thought I was rash, if not mad, to buy it – and very brave indeed to sleep there alone, as year after year, we did, my cats and I, in a happier and more silent peace than I have known elsewhere on earth.' When her money ran out and she had to return to live in England, Roundstone became her Paradise Lost.

The poet Patrick Kavanagh (1904–1967) was born at Mucker, Inniskeen, County Monaghan, in a house built as far back as 1791 as a thatched cottage but increased to two storeys after his birth. Here as a youth, while he was apprenticed to the shoemaking trade, he would write furiously in the loft of the house or in the room where the sewing-machine was kept. Remembering it later, his brother Peter wrote: 'Everywhere were sheets covered with verse. As long as I remember no evening passed that he did not write something.' Here he played football with the Inniskeen Rovers and helped on the family farm which included outlying land at Shancoduff. It was here too, after he had made his name as a poet in Dublin, that they brought him to be buried, two stones from a nearby stream put across his grave, one cut with the words: 'There were stepping stones across a stream. Part of my life was there. The happiest part.'

Notable Dublin poets include Austin Clarke (1896–1974), whose most famous home was in the Templeogue area of Dublin city; and Seamus O'Sullivan (1879–1958) whose Dublin home was always open to young writers. Another salon of that era was the girlhood home of the poet Katharine Tynan (1861–1931), Whitehall, in what was then the country area of Clondalkin, County Dublin. Here Yeats was a frequent visitor and on Sundays often as many as twenty people sat down to the main meal of the day at 4.30 pm, after which the larder, wrote Katharine, was usually as bare as Mother Hubbard's.

Finally there is Brendan Behan (1923–1964), novelist, playwright and every inch a Dubliner; a Russler, earning his name from the street where he grew up at No. 14 Russell Street, now demolished. There, as a boy, his mother filled him with nationalistic ideas and his father read to him and his brothers from Zola, Maupassant and Galsworthy. Like most modern writers he was born in a hospital; in the National Maternity Hospital on Holles Street, at the corner of Merrion Square. Though later the family moved to 70 Kildare Road, Kimmage, the gaols of the country where he served time for his IRA activities must also be considered as landmarks associated with Behan. He served time in Arbour Hill in Dublin, the Curragh Camp on the plains of County Kildare and in Mountjoy Gaol, Dublin, where he got the idea for *The Quare Fellow*. By Behan's time, the day of the salon and soirées was well and truly over but it had been amply replaced by the pubs, and Davy Byrnes, McDaids and the Pearl Bar, now gone, were among the writer's favourites. The Catacombes, a complex of cellars beneath a Georgian house in Fitzwilliam Square, frequented by students and artists of all kinds, was another of his haunts. Some time after his marriage to Beatrice Salkeld he set up house at 5 Anglesea Road, Ballsbridge, Dublin, but eventually his drinking habits caught up with him. After he died in the Meath Hospital he was buried in Glasnevin cemetery, with what seemed like half the city of Dublin following him to his grave to pay their last respects.

Today Irish writing is still at flood-time. There is no shortage of writers who live in homes of all descriptions in various parts of the country. The only reason they are not included here is because this is a book, not about the living, but about the dead.

# AE (George Russell)

## 1867-1935

Poet, playwright, painter and mystic, George Russell, known as AE, was born in William Street in Lurgan, County Armagh, and spent the first years of his life in a cottage on the estate of the Brownlow family, holders of the title Lord Lurgan. His father, Thomas Elias Russell, was a bookkeeper with Bell and Company, a Quaker firm of cambric manufacturers, but in 1878 he moved his family south, to Dublin, a change of scene for which AE was ever after thankful. Later he wrote that he had never been grateful enough to Providence for the mercy it showed by removing him from Ulster at an early age: 'Though I like the people I cannot breathe in the religious and political atmosphere of the north-east corner of Ireland.'

When in later life he returned on holidays he stayed either with his maternal grandparents on their farm at Drumgor in the vicinity of Lough Neagh, or with his father's sister who lived in one of the grey stone dwellings known as Shiels Almhouses in the Portadown Road area of the town of Armagh, which had been built in the mid-nineteenth century with funds provided by an altruist named Charles Shiels. In Armagh, with his childhood friend Carrie Rea, he often visited the Observatory to have a look at the heavens, which nourished his latent mysticism, and roamed the demesne of the Archbishop's palace where according to Carrie he first felt the impulse to write and to draw.

The family move to Dublin was the result of an invitation to Mr. Russell to join a firm of chartered accountants in Dame Street, and their first home in the city was at 33 Emorville Avenue, a modest two-storied redbrick terrace house off the South Circular Road, close to

*33 Emorville Avenue (far left)*
*67 Grosvenor Square (left)*
*Kill-o-the-Grange cemetery*
*(right)*

Clanbrassil Street. There they lived for seven years, with George first attending Dr. Power's school in Harrington Street, and later an establishment called the Rathmines School, run by Dr. C. W. Benson. Here he won all the prizes and was known as 'the genius', while one special friend, Henry Chester Browne, dubbed him 'the special artist and literary critic' of the school. These two, with another pal Henry Goodwillie, would wander about the south-side streets whenever they had an afternoon free. Another favourite haunt was the river Dodder and often as they walked beside its waters George would stop here and there to make one of his little sketches.

The Russells had three children, two boys and a girl, but while they were living at Emorville Avenue, their daughter, Mary Elizabeth, died aged eighteen. Shortly afterwards they moved to a new home, 67 Grosvenor Square, in the south-side suburb of Rathmines. Around this vicinity, of quiet well-kept squares, comfortable redbrick houses and tree-lined avenues, George often walked with his friend Willie Yeats, and it was somewhere along the length of Leinster Road that he first heard an outline for the plot of Yeats' play, *The Shadowy Waters*. He met Yeats most probably at the Metropolitan School of Art in Kildare Street which he had attended intermittently since the age of thirteen. Here too he came into contact with sculptors John Hughes and Oliver Sheppard, both of whom were to do busts of him later in life. Through Yeats, he also met the young poet, Katharine Tynan, who made him welcome at literary parties in Whitehall, her father's large house in the then rural Newlands Cross area of Clondalkin in County Dublin. Because of his interest in mysticism she thought of Russell initially as

another William Blake, and in her memoirs she wrote: 'I have known in my time some few undoubted geniuses, three certainly in literature – W. B. Yeats, Francis Thompson, and George Russell – to whom I believe I have added a fourth in James Stephens. In none of these have I found the beauty of genius as I found it in George Russell. His flame has always burnt upward clearly. There is no room in him for any of the small meannesses of humanity.'

As a young man, George attended evening classes at the school affiliated to the Royal Hibernian Academy but the Russells were not wealthy and he also had to earn a living. For most of the 1890s he worked, for £40 a year, as a clerk in the big Dublin drapery firm of Pims in South Great George's Street, starting each morning at nine and finishing at six-thirty or seven each night. There he won a reputation for being very businesslike, a model clerk who set a fine example for his colleagues. By all accounts, however, he must have been an interesting fellow worker, stopping every now and then as he did to jot down a poem, make a prophesy or have one of his visions.

By then his interest in theosophy had begun and when a Scottish engineer, Frederick Dick, and his wife established a small residential community for Theosophists at 3 Upper Ely Place, George joined them. There he took part in lectures, helped in the small library, listened when Dick played Beethoven and Chopin on the piano, and painted some mysterious-looking murals which can still be seen on the walls of the house. He also read a great deal. Later he wrote: 'The seven years I lived there were the happiest in my life. How fortunate I was to be drawn into companionship with six or seven others, all as I

29

think wiser and stronger than I then was.'

Life at Ely Place was also quite monastic, with many of the residents intending to remain celibate all their lives, but George didn't spend all his time there. He went home occasionally to stay at his parents' new home, 5 Seapoint Terrace, Monkstown, and one of his favourite places in that area was the Kill-o-the-Grange cemetery. John Eglinton, who wrote *A Memoir of AE* recalls that often, exhausted after a night's work at the National Library, he would be called off his homeward-bound train at the station near George's house so that the two could go and talk in the solitude of the cemetery. Generally, however, their meetings took place on Sunday afternoons, when they sat on the tombstones, smoking and talking, the conversation ranging from theories of high spirituality one minute, to funny incidents at Pims the next. In this setting, George read out two acts of his new play, *Deirdre.*

From the mid 1890s, George's life changed in many important ways. In 1894 he published a collection of poems, *Homeward: Songs by the Way*, under the pseudonym AE; he had actually intended it to be AEON but a careless printer omitted the last two letters. In 1897 he changed jobs. Horace Plunkett, the founder of the Irish Agricultural Organisation Society for the promotion of co-operation among the country's poor farmers, appointed AE as its organizer, based at 2 Lincoln Place, and from then on he was to travel the country widely, bringing the co-operative message to the remotest parts.

The following year, in the Dublin Registry Office, he married Violet North, a young English Theosophist who had lived for a time at 3 Upper Ely Place. They had several addresses in their early married life

– 10 Grove Terrace, 6 Castlewood Avenue and 28 Upper Mount Pleasant Avenue, all in the Rathmines area. It was a sad blow when their first-born child died, and, meeting AE at the railway station on the way home from the burial, Eglinton remembers how disconsolate the writer was, struggling to hold back his tears. The Russells were to have two more children, Brian and Diarmuid.

From the start of their married life, the Russells' home was a welcoming place, especially when they moved to 25 Coulson Avenue, Rathgar, where they had two distinguished neighbours, Maud Gonne and Countess Markiewicz. It was here, hanging about against the railings that, late one August night in 1902, AE met a tall thin young man. This was James Joyce, who had been waiting there since earlier in the evening. When AE finally appeared, the young writer enquired if it was not perhaps too late to come calling but AE, in true spirit, replied that it was never too late and invited him in. They sat up until four o'clock next morning and AE, by suggesting to Joyce that he write a story for *The Irish Homestead,* may unwittingly have been the inspirer of *Dubliners.* From 1905 on, AE edited *The Irish Homestead,* which much later became *The Irish Statesman.*

While the Russells were still living at Coulson Avenue, his play *Deirdre* was first performed by W. G. Fay's Irish National Dramatic Company at St. Teresa's Hall in Clarendon Street. Though his work kept him very much involved, he managed to write poetry on a reasonably regular basis until his death.

Of all his Dublin addresses, it is 17 Rathgar Avenue that remains most associated with him, for he lived there for over twenty-five years.

31

Dr. Monk Gibbon described him as the oracle towards which sooner or later every literary aspirant in Dublin gravitated, mostly to the Sunday evenings which began around seven-thirty in the evening. James Stephens, Seamus O'Sullivan, Austin Clarke, Padraic Colum, Frank O'Connor and Monk Gibbon were just some of those who came for tea and cake and to listen to AE, 'the greatest conversationalist I have ever met', according to James Stephens. Sometimes visitors would be brought into the studio in the front of the house first, but mostly the group sat in the back room where AE kept his library of eastern books and detective novels; when guests outnumbered the chairs, cushions were put on the floor.

Not everybody arrived at the appointed hour. Once AE arrived home late at night to find a young poet from County Monaghan waiting for him, Paddy Kavanagh. They talked about Emerson and Whitman and when Kavanagh was leaving, AE gave him some books to take back to his native Inniskeen.

AE usually took his holidays in north County Donegal, close to Sheephaven Bay, where he stayed in a hillside cottage at Breaghy or on the Marble Hill estate in a 'fairy' house originally built for children. Later he stayed at Glenveagh Castle, a baronial castle built in 1870 with a rather tragic history intertwined with evictions and deaths; while AE was staying there on one occasion his host, Professor Kingsley Porter, disappeared, presumed drowned, when visiting Inishbofin.

The writer's attitude to Donegal is summed up in a letter: 'I am off on holiday next month to Donegal in northern Ireland, to the wildest, loneliest and loveliest country I know, a country of hills and hollows, of lakes and woods, of cliffs, mountains, rivers, inlets of sea, sands, ruined castles and memories from the beginning of the world.' Another time, feeling drained after a strenuous bout of work, he wrote of how he had come back to Donegal, to 'fill the empty psyche'.

The Irish Agricultural Organisation Society had moved in 1908 to 84 Merrion Square, Plunkett House. AE had an office on the second floor and though, according to Lord Dunsany, the room was a dingy one AE had made of it 'a fairyland from floor to ceiling' with his brush. Here he received many visitors including Yeats who lived for a time in Merrion Square; this inspired the famous cartoon depicting the two writers, one en route to visit the other, so deep in their own thoughts that they passed each other in the street.

At the IAOS AE had an assistant and special friend, the poet Susan Mitchell, from Carrick-on-Shannon in County Leitrim. She lived only a block away from the Russells in Rathgar and when she died in 1926 he described it to a friend as a great blow, 'indeed the heaviest blow I ever felt in my life, because she was the kindest and most unselfish of colleagues for over twenty years'. Now he had, he added, to push his pen across the paper to get an article written: 'In the old days my thought ran before the pen'.

When his wife died in 1932, the days grew lonely for AE. He sold the house in Rathgar Avenue and lived mostly outside Ireland. But he never ceased to miss it as his letters from America show. There his life was a whirlwind of lectures, dinner engagements, photographic sessions, interviews and meetings with eminent writers, and through much of it he appears to have been a bit bewildered, moving from desert to pasture-land to the bustle of big cities. 'I am becoming fluent and brazen and in the midst of it all am pining to be back in Ireland,' he wrote; adding months later from New York: 'I will be dotting off the days now until I get back in April. Ireland here seems remote at times as the pre-war world, and seven thousand miles away like something one heard of about one's cradle very far off and long ago.'

When in England, he became ill and went into a Bournemouth nursing home. Oliver St. John Gogarty came over from Ireland, bearing messages, and word came too from Yeats, though he and AE no longer had the special closeness of their youth. He died on 17 July 1935 in the Stagsden Nursing Home, Bournemouth, surrounded by a small circle of close friends including Gogarty and John Eglinton. When his body was taken back to Dublin, three planes flew low over the water in salute as the boat came into Dublin Bay, and the coffin, laden with flowers, stood for a time in Plunkett House for the last tributes from his friends. He was buried in Mount Jerome cemetery, Eamon de Valera and Yeats being but two of the city's notable figures who walked in the throng of mourners.

Not all those at the funeral were famous, however. One woman silently placed a large bouquet of flowers on the grave. She had once worked as a servant girl with the Russells and when she became pregnant AE had not sent her away but had cared for her instead. 'I would have died for him.' she said simply by way of explanation.

*Kilkenny College*

# Michael Banim and John Banim

### 1796-1874          1798-1842

While scholars may never agree on how much Michael Banim collaborated with his younger brother John in the writing of their *Tales of the O'Hara Family* there can be no doubt about the depth of the affection between the pair, both born in Kilkenny at the close of the eighteenth century.

Michael was the older of the two and though there was talk of his going on for the bar he eventually ended up in the family business. In the beginning John had all the advantages, getting a fine education and the chance to live in Dublin. Michael, like the brothers of other famous writers, stayed in the background, collecting material for John, providing encouragement and advice, yet there was never any jealousy between them.

'The sole thing that sends the blood to my heart or the tear to my eye is the recollection that I am parted from you,' John once wrote to his brother, 'but this gives me greater strength for the struggle to get back – and back I will return, if God spares me life – and we will spend and end our days together.' And today the two do lie side by side in the overgrown and bramble-filled graveyard of St. John's church in Kilkenny. Though Michael did not die for over thirty years after his brother, he found it painful, even as an old man, to think back on the fine times they had had together long before.

The Banims were sons of a middle-class Catholic farmer who also had a sports shop in Kilkenny. John, who was born in 1798, was indulged in every way by his mother who always sat him in the best chair at mealtimes and made sure that he got the best food to eat. He reciprocated her love for him. When he was still a little fellow he became obsessed with the idea that a highwayman might one day run off with her and he would often run out of the classroom, home down the street, to check that she was still there. Mrs. Banim and John were both great readers and every so often he would take time from school to steal away out into the lanes and fields about the town to read the new romances and the latest magazines.

John went to five schools before finally arriving at Kilkenny College, the corridors of which had previously been trodden by such illustrious literary men as Swift, Farquhar, Congreve and Berkeley. When he went there he had already begun to write and to show an interest in the stage for which he was also to write later. When he was ten, a private theatre opened in the town and he was overpowered by the excitement of performances there, by the magnificently lit house, by the glamour of the audience, by the costumes and scenery. What impressed him more than anything, however, was a reading given there on one occasion by Thomas Moore. The morning after the performance he got together his own literary efforts and brought them down the town for the opinion of the great man. Moore received the small author kindly, calling him a brother poet, and years later he recognized Banim's success by leaving a visiting-card at the house when on his way through Kilkenny.

John, as a boy, also had a bent for mechanical inventions, trying once to build a sky rocket, and another time making wings for his brother and sister so that they might fly, but both episodes ended in near catastrophe.

It was, however, at art that he excelled in those early days and when he left Kilkenny College his father sent him to the drawing academy of the Royal Dublin Society in Dublin. He worked hard and visited the galleries but he was very lonely and when he qualified at the age of eighteen he went home to Kilkenny and got a job teaching art. The job must have seemed a blessing then, particularly as he shortly fell in love with one of his pupils, but it was a mixed blessing as ultimately it brought disaster on him.

The girl with whom he fell in love was the illegitimate daughter of a local squire who would not accept John Banim as her husband. He sent her away to friends where, within months, she caught consumption and died. John walked twenty-five miles in the rain and frost of November to see her before she was buried, but the family

*Inistioge
bridge near
Woodstock,
County
Kilkenny*

only abused him. Tormented and in deep despair, he wandered aimlessly through the villages and countryside until his brother found him and brought him home. Though after twelve months he seemed to have recovered, the hardship left its mark for it was during that time that he contracted the spinal tuberculosis that plagued him for the rest of his life, eventually killing him.

After his partial recovery, John became editor of the *Leinster Gazette*, and later, from Dublin, he wrote for the *Limerick Evening Post* and other papers. He still however visited home regularly where he would spend hours walking with Michael through the nearby demesne of Woodstock at Inistioge, famed for its beechwoods, planning the stories they would write. After his marriage to a local girl John like other Irish writers of the period went to London, but though he managed to write there he was constantly upset either by illness in the family or by his own ill-health. At night he was often in agony, tossing and turning in bed until he cried out with pain, and all the time he missed home. To the family he wrote: 'We must live together; that is a blessed truth. Such a set of people were not born to dwell asunder.' If they were all gathered together under one roof, he seemed to believe, perhaps the old times might come back again after all.

When his illness became worse, the doctors suggested he go to France where he tried baths, medicaments, and cures, none of which did any good and some of which his brother Michael was later convinced had done him a lot of harm. He caught cholera abroad; Ellen, his wife, was ill; and one of their babies, a little boy, died and had to be buried in Montmartre, something which his father never forgot or

ceased to be sad about. Michael wrote letters all the time, begging him to come home and he himself felt the same old yearning to be there. 'Not a very long time shall elapse if I live till we meet in Kilkenny. My wanderings, with God's leave, must end there,' he wrote to Michael.

All these tragedies had cost him money but the public was generous where John Banim was concerned. *The Times* printed an appeal on his behalf and subscriptions were entered in Dublin, Clonmel and other places. In August 1835 he sailed home. Recalling it later, Michael remembered the shock he got when he saw his young brother again; though only a man of thirty-seven he was wrinkled and grey-haired and could hardly move without assistance. 'We were not long, however, recognizing each other and renewing our old love,' he added.

To mark his return a benefit performance of his work was given in Dublin at the Theatre Royal and when, in September, he arrived in Kilkenny the people who had collected £85 on his behalf were all there to greet him. Later the Queen granted him a pension of £150 a year.

When away he had often whiled away the time dreaming of the kind of home he would like to have in Kilkenny. He wanted a house full of windows, set in a garden within sight of the Nore, and Wind Gap Cottage, his last home in the town, fits that description. With its turrets, chimneys and many gables, the little yellow-painted house, covered in wisteria, must be noticed by most drivers who pass through Kilkenny.

When he lived there most of the days were spent in the garden. He would sit there in his Bath chair enjoying the shrubs and plants, asking to be brought indoors only when the Dublin coach was passing, as the driver had a habit of pointing him out to the passengers as a curiosity.

38

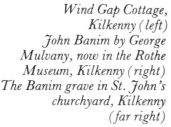

*Wind Gap Cottage,*
*Kilkenny (left)*
*John Banim by George*
*Mulvany, now in the Rothe*
*Museum, Kilkenny (right)*
*The Banim grave in St. John's*
*churchyard, Kilkenny*
*(far right)*

When not in the garden he would ride out in the post-chaise or be pushed along the country roads by his daughter Mary, in a chair with four wheels attached. Often he picked up passing strays and brought them home with him. In particular there was one young deaf and dumb boy who had either escaped or been discharged from an institution in Glasnevin in Dublin and who was pathetically grateful for Banim's interest in him. He would arrive at the house every day when they carried the writer out into the garden and silently commence to weed the flower beds and water the plants. John was also visited by loyal friends, among them the Limerick writer Gerald Griffin.

John Banim was only forty-four when he died but he looked like an old man. His life was so full of hardship that in retrospect it sounds almost like a melodrama. Michael, on the other hand, lived on for years, continuing to write, and later he became the town postmaster. John's last surviving child did not reach adulthood, but Michael's daughters carried on the family name. Though all the opportunities had been given to his younger brother when they were boys, life had been kinder to him in the end.

Today the Museum in High Street, Kilkenny, once a school the Banim brothers attended, contains a number of mementoes of them.

*Bowen's Court*

# Elizabeth Bowen

## 1899-1973

Elizabeth Bowen was only six weeks old when, on a July evening in 1899, she was first brought to Bowen's Court, the ancestral home of her forbears near Kildorrery in County Cork.

Down the upper avenue jogged the inside car, carrying Elizabeth, her nurse and her mother, Florence Bowen, proud after nine years of an infertile marriage to be bringing home an heir at last, even if it was a girl, for the family was not bound by the Salic law. Inside the house she turned up the oil-lamp in the hall so that the baby could be seen by everyone and compared with the faces in the family portraits lining the walls, and of which there were plenty for the Bowens had been in County Cork since the middle of the seventeenth century. Originally from the Gower peninsula in Wales, the Irish connection began when a Henry Bowen came to the country as a lieutenant-colonel in Cromwell's army. According to family tradition he acquired his land in a most romantic way.

He had two pet hawks of which he was very fond, but during an altercation with Cromwell, the latter wrung the neck of one of the birds, killing it. He made up the rift by offering Bowen as much Irish land as the other hawk could fly over before coming down. And so, set off by its master from the foot of the Ballyhouras mountains, the bird flew south, winning for the Bowens over eight hundred acres of land around the hamlet of Farahy. This story was later invalidated for Elizabeth when she was told that a hawk flies straight up and hangs in the air until it drops on its prey, but be that as it may the bird remained the Bowen family crest.

For the next century the family lived in a number of houses in the

41

area. It was not until 1775 that the Colonel's great-great-grandson, another Henry, completed Bowen's Court, the limestone house described by Elizabeth as being severely classical outside and very bare inside. Its most remarkable feature was the windows which gave the entire house the impression of being flooded with light. With its high long rooms, Bowen's Court dictated a certain formality, but it had a special place for levity as well: 'Any casual life goes on on the front steps; in summer, when there is sunshine, when there are visitors, these, strewn with cushions, deck chairs, papers and books, take on a *villeggiatura* air.'

When Elizabeth first arrived at Bowen's Court, there were no doting grandparents to meet her. Both were dead. Around 1881 there had been an outbreak of smallpox and one of the children, Henry, who became Elizabeth's father, caught the disease; his mother died after nursing him back to health. His father survived her by only seven years, dying in 1888. In the years that followed, a daughter, Sarah, kept house at Bowen's Court for her younger brothers and sisters, with only two servants to help her. Shortly after Henry's marriage, to Florence Colley of Clontarf in Dublin, the remaining family moved away to live in the nearby town of Mitchelstown.

Henry, unlike his landlord ancestors, also had a career as a barrister in Dublin, so Elizabeth was born at his home there, in 15 Herbert Place, a house on a quiet leafy street overlooking the Grand Canal, which, because summers were always spent at Bowen's Court, she grew up thinking of as a winter house only. 'Early dusks, humid reflections, and pale sunshine seemed a part of its being,' she wrote in *Seven Winters*, her nostalgic memoir of those first seven years in Herbert Place.

The finest room in the house was the drawing-room, decorated in green, with moiré wallpaper and leaf-patterned Morris tapestry curtains. There, reflected in the Florentine mirrors, stood the piano and the Chesterfield sofa on which Florence reclined when *enceinte* with Elizabeth, passing the days stroking her cat Tory and eating innumerable raisins in the firm belief that they would benefit both herself and the child.

This was the room to which Elizabeth was brought down to see her mother, particularly on Sunday evenings. Family and friends would be gathered and, after tea, the candles on the piano lit and hymns sung,

*Herbert Place, the
terrace of houses and the
canal that flows past
beyond the road:
No. 15 (below) is
the house on the right*

the last one being always *Shall We Gather By The River?* because that was the child's special favourite.

Most of her time, however, was spent in the nursery above, a blue-grey room lined with pictures from the nursery rhymes. There many a time the future writer tossed and turned, unable to sleep during the noontime nap. There, too, she would be stood in front of the fire when going out to a party, to be dressed in lace and jewellery like all the other little girls. In Elizabeth's case, the jewellery was either a heart-shaped locket on a gold chain or a shamrock brooch with pearl attached.

One regular event each week was the trip to Miss Thieler's day-time dancing class in the Molesworth Hall in Molesworth Street, through the windows of which long dazzling shafts of sunshine would fall if the day was fine. There on the hall's scrubbed floor boards the little girls in their white muslins, sandals and open-work stockings would twirl this way and that, under the approving eye of nurses, mothers and governesses. Occasionally one would get a chance to take a turn on the boards with a certain Fergus, one of Miss Thieler's star pupils who wore an Eton suit, possessed charm and had the unmistakable air of being a man of the world.

On other days, in her scarlet coat and tam-o'-shanter, she would be taken for walks by the governess around the south side of the city which to her had the spaciousness of a *banlieue*. In St. Stephen's Green and the streets around Leinster House, sometimes when sun fell on the houses, mews and laneways of that district, it made her think that Dublin was sealing up all the sunshine, just as an unopened orange

*Mount Temple, Clontarf.*
*An avenue leads up to the*
*entrance front (left),*
*the back looks out to*
*Dublin bay*

would seal up juice. Her walks were not always taken alone. Among her companions were Humphrey Fane Vernon who lived in Wilton Place and taught her how to stand on her head, and the long-haired Noel Summers who had the distinction of staying at Clontarf Castle. There were also the Townshend boys who like her, wore scarlet coats. Best of all, however, there was her cousin Vernie Cole, who was a fount of ideas and facts. He was, she recalled, small, thin, fair, pink-tipped and energetic, always dressed in a fawn-coloured coat and cap. It was Vernie who did his best to teach his golden-haired cousin German.

There were regular shopping expeditions to Upper Baggot Street; to the victuallers with the sawdust on the floor, to the chemist shop with its stock of green and violet bottles, and the drapery where the yards of material that hung on high made it appear to the child's eye as mysterious as a Moorish tent. Nearby the bakery gave out the unmistakable aroma of spicy cakes and bread, and in every shop the staff knew the names of all their regular customers. 'Everyone had not only manners but time; we nearby residents made this our own village,' she recalled.

Sundays were inevitably spent at Mount Temple, the big, gabled, Victorian home in Clontarf of her maternal grandparents, the Colleys. There in the house that looked out over lawns to the sea, Bitha, as Elizabeth was called, would be affectionately inspected by well-meaning aunts and uncles. On Sundays she wore not only a white muff and coat but a white saucer-shaped hat with an ostrich feather peeping out over the brim.

During this early childhood, her father had left the Law Library and

45

gone to work in the Land Commission. Perhaps because of the long hours he worked there, he developed a mental illness described by his daughter as anaemia of the brain, and had to go for treatment to England. Separation from his wife and child was also prescribed and from then on, seven-year-old Bitha lived in England with her mother, in various places on the coast of Kent – Folkestone, Lyminge, Seabrook and Hythe. Though after some years Mr. Bowen recovered and came back to live with them, they were not long to be a family unit, for in the intervening years, Florence had become ill with cancer and in 1912 she died. For her thirteen-year-old daughter it was a terrible blow, for theirs had been a most loving relationship: 'She gave me – most important of all as a start in life – the radiant confident feeling of being loved.'

From then on Elizabeth was brought up by various relations on both sides of the Irish Sea, but chiefly by her mother's spinster sister, Laura, at Harpenden in England, and her uncle, George Colley, at Corkagh House in Clondalkin, Dublin. But she was never long away from Bowen's Court where possibly her favourite spot was the garden. Covering three acres, enclosed by a wall, it was filled mostly with old-fashioned flowers, with jonquils, moss roses, sweet pea, and with voluminous peonies in crimson and white. In the middle was a sun-dial and two bushes of Caroline allspice. Elsewhere was the tennis court and a shady corner in which tea would be taken, weather permitting. Her usual companions on these visits were her cousin, Audrey Fiennes, and her father who eventually became well enough to marry for the second time; his bride was Mary Gwynn of Clontarf.

When they grew older, Audrey and Elizabeth went to garrison and country house dances in the locality and once gave a ball themselves at Bowen's Court. It was a romantic time and Elizabeth was soon engaged to one John Anderson, a British army lieutenant, but the engagement did not last long. It was also, though they did not then know it, the end of an era. Long afterwards she remembered the day when her father, who was escorting them to a garden party at Mitchelstown Castle, stopped the pony at Rockmills and in the local post-office heard the news that England had declared war on Germany. At the party the band played and the guests ate their ices but everyone was talking of war. It was, she later wrote, a more final scene than they knew: 'Ten years hence, it was all to seem like a dream – and the Castle itself would be a few bleached stumps on the plateau. Today, the terraces are obliterated, and grass grows where the saloons were. Many of these guests, those vehement talkers, would be scattered, houseless, sonless or themselves dead. That war – or call it now that first phase of war – was to go far before it had done with us.'

After the war came the Irish 'troubles'. One spring night during the War of Independence, three big houses in the vicinity of Bowen's Court – Rockmills, Ballywalter and Convamore – were all burned, and her father wrote warning her to prepare for the worst. However, Bowen's Court escaped then and also in the Civil War that followed, even though at one point it was occupied by a party of Republicans who spent some days there, mining the avenue and making preparations to blow up the house, before departing and leaving it unharmed.

In 1923 Elizabeth married Alan Cameron, an Englishman, and though they had no children the marriage was a successful one. Seven years later she inherited Bowen's Court and in time made improvements, putting in bathrooms and electricity, refurbishing the drawing-room with new pink satin curtains. Among the many guests there over the summers were the writers Carson McCullers and Rosamond Lehmann.

When her husband retired in 1952, they moved permanently to Bowen's Court but they were only to have the spring and summer there before he died unexpectedly. For seven years she tried to maintain the place, but costs were rising and anxiety over the future slowed down her creative powers. 'Matters reached a crisis. By 1959 it had become inevitable that I should sell Bowen's Court,' she wrote of what was perhaps the saddest decision of her life. When she did sell – to a local man – the house that had withstood both war and burnings, was demolished. Down came the limestone facade, its ceilings wrought by Italian plasterworkers, and the window pane on which Elizabeth's name had once been scratched by the edge of her mother's diamond ring. It was also the end of the Long Room where once deck tennis and French cricket had been played on wet days, and of which she had written: 'When one returns to Bowen's Court after an absence one never feels one has really come home again until one has been up to the Long Room.' Up the avenue of Bowen's Court the tenants had pulled her parents' bridal carriage years before, and on its kitchen table jigs had been danced when she herself was born. Now it was all over. Never again at Christmas-time would the ritual Bowen's Court candle, pink or green, light a path over the fields from Christmas Eve through Twelfth Night.

The house having played its part, had come to an end, she concluded: 'The shallow hollow of land, under the mountains, on which Bowen's Court stood is again empty. Not one hewn stone left on another on the fresh growing grass. Green covers all traces of the foundations. Today, as far as the eye can see, there might never have been a house there.' Her only consolation was that at least the house had had a clean end: 'Bowen's Court never lived to be a ruin.'

She came over from England a few times more, to wander through the vacant grounds. When she died she was buried in Farahy churchyard, the graveyard that she had once called elegiac, where Catholics and Protestants, landlords and tenants, lie together in undisputed peace, and where, in summer, the trees bend their branches low over the graves.

*The gate lodge at Mount Temple*

# William Carleton

## *1794-1869*

William Carleton, the writer Daniel O'Connell would call the Walter Scott of Ireland and with whom, in the judgement of W. B. Yeats, modern Irish literature began, was born in a most humble setting, the youngest boy of fourteen children of a small farmer in the townland of Prillisk near Clogher in County Tyrone. But though the place of his birth may have been only a fourteen-acre holding, it was rich in other ways: 'My native place was a spot rife with old legends, tales, traditions, customs and superstitions, so that in my early youth, even beyond the walls of my own humble roof, they met me in every direction.'

While he was still a child they moved to a place called Tonagh, known locally as Towney, but he liked their next home at Nurchasy near Findermore better: 'Nurchasy to me was paradise. The view from it of Fardress Glen, so beautifully wooded, and of Fardress grazing fields, so green and extensive, together with the effect of those small circular groves peculiar to some portions of the north absolutely enchanted me.' Though he cried when they left Nurchasy, their next home at Springtown had an attraction of its own. It was beside a hazel glen: 'This was alive with blackbirds and thrushes, and upon a fine, calm summer evening was vocal in a hundred places with their melody.'

It was in Springtown, at Mass one Sunday, that he first saw Anne Duffy, the miller's daughter from nearby Augher, whom long afterwards he still called his first and most enthusiastic love. Though they never spoke in all the four years that he knew her their eyes occasionally met and he harboured hopes for their future even though

*Dublin from Phoenix Park (left) Marino Crescent (right) – No. 2 is the centre house Marsh's Library (far right)*

his impoverished circumstances made it impossible to declare his love. It was a terrible blow when he heard she was to be married and in the barn at Springtown he wept bitter tears. When later, as a successful writer, he made a triumphant visit to County Tyrone he met Anne Duffy again and she confessed that she too had been in love with him, causing him to write in a letter that he felt as if his very heart had been divided in two.

He left his native county in his early twenties to try his luck in the world and after a rambling journey arrived in Dublin with only 2/9d in his pocket but with thoughts of *Gil Blas*, the picaresque hero of the Lesage novel, in his head. As a gypsy fortune-teller had foretold years before, he had finally arrived in the city where he would become a great man. If such a thing as the turning point in a man's life exists it happened to Carleton at that moment in 1818. For though he did not know it then he had left behind for ever the world of the Catholic Irish peasantry, of thatched cabins, hedge schools and poverty. He was to go back home on visits and the best of his writing would be about this old background but henceforth his own life would be completely changed. He would achieve fame, become a Protestant and make money, but unfortunately for him, not overnight.

In fact, his first night in Dublin was spent in a place with the ignoble name of Dirty Lane, now Bridgefoot Street. Though at first he could afford lodgings, he had eventually to resort to a flop-house along with all the beggars and con-men of the streets, an experience which was so appalling that even years later when writing his autobiography it pained him to think back over those days.

During those youthful times in Dublin he passed his days in Marsh's Library, in the public galleries of the theatres, or wandering about the south side, marvelling at the fine squares and majestic buildings. Though lack of finance meant that he had to return every evening to the poorer quarters, his resting-places were never dull. At one, in Mary's Lane, the landlady fancied the young northerner. From another in Moore Street he once had to abscond without paying. Best of all was his period in Francis Street where there was a circulating library in his room, filled with what he considered to be obscene books, including one with the intriguing title of *The Irish Female Jockey Club*. Though he was horrified at the content of these books he nevertheless spent between twelve and sixteen hours a day reading them and excused himself later by commenting that even the best of us had a taste for a bit of scandal now and then.

Needless to say, his initial capital of under three bob did not last for ever. It was augmented, first by a gift from a shoemaker with the same name as himself, and later by various jobs as amanuensis, clerk and teacher. It was at a school run by Mr. Fox, in the Coombe, that he met Jane Anderson whom he loved and married and who became the mother of his children.

One of their first homes in the city was a thatched cottage by the sea at Dollymount in a place called The Sheds but later the family moved to Clontarf. O'Donoghue, Carleton's biographer, gives the address as 2 Marino Crescent. Carleton himself, on his letter-heads, called the house 2 Clontarf Crescent, all of which seems to indicate that he did indeed live at the magnificent half moon of houses overlooking a park on the north shore of Dublin Bay, where later the writer Bram Stoker had a home. Doubt however is cast on this by Wilmot Harrison in his book *Memorable Dublin Houses* which gives Carleton's north Dublin address as 3 Marino Terrace, Fairview. One thing is certain; it was while living in this area that Carleton got word, in 1848, that he had been awarded a pension from the Queen. The citation acknowledged that it was for 'the high position which you have attained in literature and the distinguished ability with which you have illustrated the character of your country'. He was by now the author of *Traits and Stories of the Irish Peasantry*, *Rody the Rover* and many other books.

The pension, amounting to £200 a year, meant that the family could move house again, their new home being 1 Rathgar Avenue, which has since been demolished. Around this area he wandered looking, as a contemporary recorded, like a northern peasant farmer, ill at ease in his glossy hat and broadcoat. Here he was happy in the midst of his children, Mary, Anne, Rose, Sizzy, Willy, Mag and the others, for possibly more than anything else Carleton was a family man, most content when he was listening to his daughters sing around the piano, or escorting them, on his arm, to a dance at a neighbour's house. It has been said that he so feared them being buffetted about by life that he never really equipped them to go forth into it, preferring them to stay close by him instead. Even after they married he loved if choice or circumstance brought them home again – complete with husbands, wives and children. From his letters it is easy to see that there was nothing he liked better than to kiss and cuddle a small grandchild in his arms.

By now Carleton, with a lengthening list of books, was famous in Dublin and had occasionally to travel to London on business. But when away loneliness usually overcame him; he wrote letters to the family daily, had ghastly nightmares about the children and constantly wished himself back in Rathgar. Once in London he wrote that he felt 'more alone in the midst of this roar and bustle that if I were in the bosom of the remotest solitude'.

There were, of course, compensations. He loved the busy Thames and the company of literary figures like Leigh Hunt, Thackeray and Scott, but he did not relish the thought of living there, a possibility that was once on the horizon. 'I think it very likely that we shall all come here,' he wrote to Sizzy, but 'I confess that it would go near to break my heart to leave the glorious views which we have from our drawing-room window, to which there is nothing at all comparable in or about London. Brick walls, magnificent buildings, rich and gorgeous shops, crowds eternally passing and repassing – all this, and a thousand times more, is here; but then it is all art, and I fear that if I were taken away from my sea and my green fields, and the natural influence and beautiful change of the seasons – which cannot be seen or felt here – I fear, I say again, that if I were deprived of these, I would wither like a tree too old to be transplanted, and after a little drooping would die.'

His own fields, hills, valleys and mountains; how could he leave them now, he asked, knit as they were into his heart? And how could he, he also lamented, leave the land in which all belonging to him lay sleeping? But they did not go that time, nor did they leave Ireland later for Canada, though Carleton was sorely tempted to do so as three of his daughters had gone there to make their lives, for a time.

Gavan Duffy, then in Australia, dissuaded him from emigrating. 'Do not dream of Canada, my friend; an oak of the forest will not bear transplanting,' he wrote, adding that even a shrub like himself did not at once take kindly to a new climate and soil. The slopes of Howth, the hills of Wicklow, and the friends of manhood were not, he said, to be matched even in such a golden land as Australia.

So Carleton stayed in Ireland, living out his last years at 2 Woodville in the Sandford Road area of Ranelagh, where he socialized with both the Jesuits from Milltown Park and the Protestant clergy from the nearby church. So celebrated was he by then in the city that a letter addressed simply 'William Carleton, author of *The Poor Scholar*, Dublin', reached him without difficulty. But the years also brought tragedy; he lived to see his favourite daughter, Rose, die of cancer.

Carleton's grave is in Mount Jerome cemetery where the inscription proclaims that therein lie the remains of one 'whose memory needs neither gravestone nor sculptured marble to preserve it from oblivion'.

# Lord Dunsany

## 1878-1957

One night in 1912, when the eighteenth Lord Dunsany was addressing the National Literary Society at its Dublin headquarters in St. Stephen's Green, one of the assembled company asked him if he really believed anything good could come out of County Meath. Some of those present apparently thought that Meath, the county of beef cattle and big farmers, was not a conducive background to the production of poetry, but Lord Dunsany disagreed. That county if any, he assured them, was the most favourable to the production of high-spirited things. Did its people not live under the shadow of Tara? Was not the dust of the best of Ireland's kings under their feet?

In view of all this it is surprising to discover that Lord Dunsany was born, not in Meath but on a leafy square in the Regent's Park area of London, where one of his earliest memories was that of sun lighting up the first marigolds of summer. As a boy, though schooldays were spent at Cheam and Eton, he often holidayed at what he called his grandfather's Irish place, Dunsany Castle in County Meath. Founded around 1200 by Hugh de Lacy, one of the leaders of the Norman invasion, the castle and the neighbouring castle of Killeen passed, in 1403, by marriage to Sir Christopher Plunkett. Killeen was subsequently left to his eldest son, ancestor of the Earls of Fingall, and Dunsany to his second son who became the first Baron of Dunsany. The ivy-clad castle, which has been added to over the centuries, is without a doubt one of the most beautiful houses associated with a writer in Ireland.

It was here that Eddie Plunkett, as the future Lord Dunsany then was, learned to shoot under the tutelage of the castle gamekeeper, Joseph Reid, and though he didn't like the sport at first it was in time

*Dunsany Castle*

13. And into Anatolia to be
    I went to shoot woodcock at Karaca-Bey
  A village nurtured by antiquity
    And clinging to it still ...
    That not one house in it survived the day
  Shone level ... fifteen years ago
    Doubt it is over. We made a fortnight's stay
  In a small house at the street's end, the sun
  Was down upon the hills, & floods stretched far below.

14. There we played chess each evening, a great stove
    Draws us holding back the bitter cold.
  His brother sat beside & watched each move
    And sometimes found a letter, which he told
    After the game was over. Then the cloth
  Of turkish poets, into English or
  Transmuted, was brought out, & songs of old
  Gleamed in that evening, for the poet's lore
  Thus from the long-lost years bright moments can restore.

15. There was a sheepfold by the house, & there
    Under our window when the night grew late
  And stilly, frozen from his mountain lair
    The wolf prowled past: our spaniels with innate
    Knowledge that he & all his ordered state
  Was enemy, called out & called again,
    Lest man should sleep unwarned. Next day the great
  Floods were still nearer to the level plains
  In one wide gleaming lake, threatened with still more rain.

16. Over the village street the geese flew low,
  Their voices mingling with the ... of men
  Of willows marked a stream's course thro' a fen
  But no more streams were seen ... & then
  The last of light was fading from the sky
    We had ourselves by flooded oak ... Then
  I heard the ... wings & various cry
  Of all the different ducks that sailed in darkness by.

17. Of an old fisherman whose feet were lost
    This story by the stove that night I heard.
  And many my readers all avoid the cost
    Of such ill luck; the old man was a Kurd
    And this was how the accident occurred.
  He stole, when he was younger & self-willed,
    A girl from the Circassians, & the word
  Went round that they objected, so he killed
  Their chief & with his limbs a good-sized basket filled.

18. The basket with the chief cut up in bits
    He left one night by a Circassian's door.
  And then, to be beyond the reach of crits,
    Took to the hills; I should have said before
    He was by trade a brigand; & no more
  Was heard of the dispute, until one day
    A whole battalion, as the old man swore,
  From Istanbul came to Karaca-Bey
  And traitors vile gave his hiding-place away.

*The library (above left)*
*Lord Dunsany's handwriting (below left)*
*Bust of Lord Dunsany (right)*

to become one of his life's great passions. Often with him in those boyhood days was a cousin, John Hawksley, and together the pair would play at navigation on a stream running through the demesne, using as vessels little wooden boats made specially by the carpenter.

The winter after Eddie left Sandhurst he came home to Dunsany on a sad mission, to carry his father's coffin to a vault near the old ruined chapel that stands in the castle grounds. Here his father would lie beside many other Dunsanys including the ancestor who built the chapel and whose image is carved in stone on the top of his tomb. When his own time came, however, Dunsany would not be buried here but in England. 'I want to be buried in Kent in the churchyard of Shoreham so as to share with every one of my neighbours whatever may be coming, when dead, as I shared it through the summer of 1940, when alive,' he wrote by way of explanation. Dunsany's English country home, Dunstall Priory, was near Shoreham.

Lord Dunsany had many great friends at Dunsany, chief among these being Francis Ledwidge, the young poet, also from Meath, whose gifts he originally discovered and whose reputation he did so much to establish. In the library the two worked on Ledwidge's poems, correcting grammar and perfecting technique, with Dunsany selecting which ones should be sent to publishers, he himself writing the letters of introduction. Nor was Ledwidge the only writer to travel up the long avenue to the castle. Others who came were Yeats and Lady Gregory, Shaw and Oliver St. John Gogarty. In later years, the short story writer Mary Lavin was to benefit greatly from Dunsany's friendship.

But of all the activities enjoyed by the writer when on the estate, it was the cricket played every August, sometimes running into September, that he loved most. In *My Ireland,* he wrote: 'One field of mine, in between two woods, has always a lonely look to me, especially at evening; most of all on a fine summer's evening with the sun still in the sky; for it is a cricket field, and the late light of warm days always reminds me of old cricket matches, when the excitement was increasing with every over and the umpires would soon draw stumps.' In those summers men came out to play from cavalry regiments stationed at the Curragh, from battalions quartered in Dublin, and from such teams as the Free Foresters. In his autobiography he wrote: 'What a team I could raise if from the mists at evening that come up white from the river I could call the ghosts of eleven of the best men with whom I have played on this ground.' Sundays were reserved for village cricket and later with nostalgia he also recalled those long sun-filled afternoons when the local men would be out on the field, their families taking tea nearby at a tent erected specially for the day.

Perhaps the most memorable summer of all at Dunsany was the summer of 1914: 'I played a little more cricket at Dunsany, and elsewhere with the Shulers, and Ledwidge continued to send me new poems, and summer shone on a world that was all at peace; but the sands of that world were running out, and were almost gone.' During the war he served with the Royal Inniskilling Fusiliers and among other postings he fought in the north of France where his young friend Ledwidge was killed.

Another of Dunsany's Irish pastimes was hunting. He was Master of the Tara Harriers, and he also hunted with the Meath, the Ward, and other hunts from counties Kildare, Dublin and Louth. Among his most memorable horses were Ardsallagh, Biscay, and a favourite one, Festina Lente, named for the family motto.

In the last ten years of his life, though the castle had been signed over to his only child, Randal, the writer still visited Dunsany often, and it was in Ireland, at a Dublin nursing home, that he died after an appendix operation from which he never recovered consciousness. After the funeral in England a memorial service was held at Kilmessan in County Meath at which, by his own request, *Crossing the Bar* was read.

# Maria Edgeworth

## 1768-1849

In December 1802, when Maria Edgeworth was living with her family for a short time in the Rue de Lille in Paris, she received what is generally understood to have been the only proposal of marriage in her life. It came from forty-six-year-old Chevalier Edelcrantz of Sweden but almost immediately Maria refused him. 'I think nothing could tempt me to leave my own dear friends and my own country to live in Sweden,' she wrote to relatives at home in Ireland. Though in the Chevalier she recognised a man of superior understanding and mild manners and though she felt for him both esteem and gratitude, she could not conceive of leaving her home for the Court of Stockholm to which he was attached. After a breakfast meeting together in Paris a few weeks after the proposal, the two parted, never to meet again.

It was not, however, the end of the story. Maria had been in love with Edelcrantz and suffered long afterwards over his memory, for according to her stepmother, Frances Edgeworth: 'The unexpected mention of his name, or even that of Sweden, in a book or a newspaper, always moved her so much that the words and lines in the page became a mass of confusion before her eyes, and her voice lost all power.'

Maria, who loved Ireland more than marriage, was not born there but in England, at the home of her maternal grandfather Paul Elers, son of a German immigrant who had married an heiress of the Hungerford family and lived on her estate in Black Bourton in Oxfordshire. Their daughter, Anna Maria Elers, married Richard Lovell Edgeworth of Edgeworthstown House, Edgeworth, County Longford. Though the marriage had been a romantic one, contracted when both

*Edgeworthstown House in the nineteenth century (left) and in 1968 (right)*

were very young, it was never really happy. As her mother died at an early age, Maria's memories of her were very vague. In later years, all she could recall were the tearful blue eyes of a sad pale lady who sometimes wore red, and to whose bedside she was summoned one day for a farewell kiss. From then on, her father became the most important person in her life. Throughout her career he would encourage and edit her writings, while she acted as his agent and accounts-keeper, and helped to educate the majority of his twenty-two children. In all, Richard Lovell had four wives; Maria's mother, Anna Maria Elers; Honora Sneyd; her sister Elizabeth; and finally Frances Beaufort who survived him.

On her father's side, Maria was the descendant of one Francis Edgeworth who had come to Ireland in 1585. About twenty-five years later he was given a grant of 600 acres around the town of Mostrim, now Edgeworthstown, in the midland county of Longford, as part of the policy of King James I of settling English Protestants on lands confiscated from Irish Catholics. In the beginning the family lived in the castle of Crannelagh near Edgeworthstown, going each summer to a residence at Kilshrewly in the same county, but both were subsequently destroyed by fire. By the early eighteenth century, a house was built at Edgeworthstown by Maria's grandfather, who structured it from one chimney that survived of a former building.

During Maria's early life, the family lived in England and it was not until she was fifteen that she came to live in Edgeworthstown on a permanent basis. Her first mature impressions of the house where she was to live almost all her life were unforgettable; though it was June, there

was snow on the roses in the garden when they arrived. She grew to love the place best in spring and early summer when the lilacs and laburnums were in bloom and when, from the upstairs windows, she could see the peonies and rhododendrons in the garden below.

The Edgeworths were substantial landlords and Richard Lovell threw himself enthusiastically into the management of his estates, seeking to build up a relationship with his tenants by doing away with middlemen and collecting the rents himself. In his spare time he worked on his inventions which included an early model of the telegraph and an attempt to create a wooden horse capable of jumping stone walls. He was the head of a happy and ever-increasing family, once boasting to a friend that neither tears nor the voice of reproof nor the hand of restraint were regular events in his house. It was in this environment that Maria began her career as a writer. She wrote virtually all her books at Edgeworthstown, including *Castle Rackrent*, *Tales of Fashionable Life*, *Patronage* and *Ormond*. Though in her lifetime she knew such literary figures as Lord Byron and Madame Récamier and was visited in County Longford by Sir Walter Scott and Wordsworth, she was essentially a home-lover with no desire to travel abroad. The world she loved best was that contained in the house at Edgeworthstown.

From the family memoirs garnered together in *The Black Book of Edgeworthstown* we have a vivid description of what the house was like in Maria's day. It had big comfortable rooms full of books, maps and clocks, and the central hall, with its stuffed birds and curiosities brought home from abroad, was hung with family portraits: 'Drawing-

room there never was in that house; the family room was the library, where all the family read and drew and worked together round the long centre table, with Maria's little desk table in a corner.' Initially she worked at a desk made specially for her by her father but later she used one that had been his, with what her stepmother Frances called many ingenious contrivances such as a bracket for her candlestick and special places for her papers. Though the library was almost always filled with the chatter of the younger children, Maria, to the astonishment of visitors to Edgeworthstown, was able to work away there on her novels, apparently undisturbed by all the commotion.

According to the *Black Book*, the upstairs of the house was just as crowded: 'Up the curving staircase crowned by a glass dome was a labyrinth of bedrooms of all sizes, the smallest being Maria's.' Even with the addition of the little bow window added by her father, of which she was so proud, the room can hardly have measured ten feet square, and it was generally shared with a sister! 'Higher up still was a series of attics inhabited by the smaller children and the servants, while the basement of the house was also thronged with people . . . Down in the depths below, a miscellaneous army of retainers worked in semi-darkness in a huge kitchen and offices, low-roofed and mud-floored . . .' Even as late as 1864, when this was written, cocks and hens were still allowed to roam at will through the kitchens.

The same memoir also gives a sketch of the garden: 'The lawn, as it was called, contained many fine trees and had a path all round it, said to measure a mile, where endless family walks were taken. There were rich grazing fields, a wood haunted by herons and known as the

*Pakenham Hall, now Tullynally Castle (left), Castle Forbes (right)*

"cranery", a quarry and a great walled fruit garden, all combining to make a demesne, in no wise remarkable, but a very pleasant spot which old and young loved and enjoyed – a homely oasis in the quiet and not very interesting country that surrounds it, and a fit setting for the plain, rambling old house that stands in its midst.'

At Edgeworthstown Maria rose early, had a cup of coffee and a glance at her post before breakfast and then worked until lunch. After that she would do needlework, occasionally going out in the carriage. 'Sometimes in the afternoons she drove out, always sitting with her back to the horses, and when quite at ease about them, exceedingly enjoying a short drive in an open carriage, not caring and often not knowing which road she went, talking and laughing all the time,' wrote Frances Beaufort. In the evenings, Maria would write some more and read aloud with the family. Occasionally too there would be visits to Castle Forbes, home of Lord Granard at Newtownforbes, to the Pakenham family at Pakenham Hall, now Tullynally Castle, Castlepollard, in County Westmeath; and now and then further afield to Black Castle, near Navan, home of Maria's aunt, Mrs. Margaret Ruxton.

This pleasant world was shattered in 1817, by the biggest blow that could have befallen her, the death of her father. Years before, conscious of the unusual bond between the pair, Chevalier Edelcrantz said that he would never be content to be loved second to a father and Richard Lovell reciprocated Maria's affection, though just how much he was probably unaware until he lay dying. No daughter since the creation of the world, he assured her, had ever given a father more

63

pleasure. So ill was Maria when the end finally came that she had to be nursed back to health by Mrs. Ruxton.

She lived on for over thirty years after her father's death, writing and carrying out altruistic projects of all kinds. When the people were starving during the famine years of 1847–1848, though she was then a very old lady, she worked constantly for their relief, writing everywhere begging for meal, for bread, for grain, and few of her requests were in vain. One donation which particularly pleased her came from the children of Boston and consisted of £150 worth of rice and flour; with it was the message, 'To Miss Edgeworth for her poor'.

Maria was over eighty when she died. She was survived by her stepmother, Frances Beaufort, whom she loved dearly and who wrote of her: 'She was gone, and nothing like her can we ever see again in this world.'

Maria is buried with her forbears in the little churchyard at Edgeworthstown.

*The church and rectory at
Edgeworthstown*

# Oliver St. John Gogarty

*1878-1957*

---

Surgeon and senator, poet, playwright and pilot, Oliver St. John Gogarty was a many-faceted man, a true native son of the city of Georgian squares and Palladian architecture which he considered to be one of the most beautiful in Europe. 'Dublin. Dublin of the vistas', he described it.

He was born at 5 Rutland Square east, on the north side; the grandest of all the Dublin squares, according to the writer, home to peers, bishops, and members of parliament, or as he later put it, to 'many worthies'. Completed in the 1770s, the square had then and still has today two focal points. The first is Charlemont House, built for James Caulfield, the Earl of Charlemont, and now the home of the Municipal Gallery of Modern Art. At the other side of the square, facing down the old Sackville Street, now O'Connell Street, is the Rotunda Hospital designed by the renowned German architect, Richard Cassels. Of this environment Gogarty wrote: 'I was probably born in my mother's room which looked out east at the backs of the houses in North Great George's Street which, though not as good an address as Rutland Square, held many distinguished persons including the great Sir John Pentland Mahaffy, afterwards Provost of Dublin University or Trinity College as it is also called. John Dillon, the patriot, had a house there and there dwelt Sir Samuel Ferguson whose poems and influence are responsible for the so-called Irish Renaissance.' Rutland Square is today Parnell Square, named after another famous man from the generation preceding Gogarty, Charles Stewart Parnell.

Gogarty's family background was a distinguished one. On his

mother's side he was descended from the Olivers of Galway, a family of prosperous millers whose ancestors were the Norman family of de Burgo. His father's family, on the other hand, were an old Gaelic clan, and though the professions had been generally barred to Catholics under the penal laws of the eighteenth century, there had been three generations of Gogarty doctors before his birth.

On the square as a small boy Oliver loved to watch the sunlight when it danced on the ceilings of the house, and to play in the back garden with his sister Mayflo and brothers Henry and Richard. Full of evergreens, the garden was particularly beautiful in early summer when pink blossom and flowering wild currants made a fragrant appearance. Beyond the garden was a stable where their father kept a hunter which he rode in the Phoenix Park. Sometimes young Oliver would be mounted too and one of his earliest memories was sitting up there, holding on tight to the reins.

Later Dr. Gogarty bought a seventeenth-century manor house, Fairfield, where Dean Swift was once said to have carved an epigram on a window in praise of a servant girl. Close to the Botanic Gardens in the north-side suburb of Glasnevin, it had its own orchard and kitchen garden as well as a cluster of hazel trees and two mulberry bushes which in season reddened the lawns with the berries that fell in abundance from their branches. In the borders of the garden grew mullien and digitalis, bryony and thyme and lily of the valley. It was to young Oliver, 'the most wonderful garden I ever saw', a place filled with peace. 'On the east side a stone wall topped with foxgloves, red and white, self sown from the herbarium beneath, let the sun flood in from over the bay and stipple the dark yew hedge with points of morning gold.' he remembered. The house was also near the Tolka river. 'The Tolka is my earliest memory of a river. By its banks, on its islands and in its waters I spent many happy days.' Here, with a band of other small boys, he would watch the pinkeens and minnows dart this way and that, and fish with bent hooks for gudgeon. Sometimes they would see a trout or a rare kingfisher, 'a blaze of bluish green', skimming along the water before disappearing into a hedge. The family also went often to stay with Dr. Gogarty's friend, Farrell O'Reilly, at Kilbeg near Kells, County Meath, and of this place and Fairfield Oliver wrote: 'Both country places put a soul into me that is made of waters, fields and trees, with a background of fairyland not too

far away.' Fairfield was years later the birthplace of his own eldest son, Oliver Duane Gogarty. It was sold in 1912 and has long since been demolished.

As a boy Gogarty went to school at North Richmond Street because it was run by the Christian Brothers whom his father believed were the best educators in Ireland. When he was thirteen his father died of a burst appendix and though this did not quite inaugurate the era of misery and servitude he later described, it did mean that the butler and some other servants had to go. It also led to Oliver being bundled off to a series of Jesuit boarding-schools, the first being Mungret College outside Limerick city which he disparagingly described as being 'a third-rate boarding-school'. Later came Stoneyhurst in England which he attended for five years. As he had a year to spare between leaving there and going to college, he was sent last of all to Clongowes Wood College at Sallins, County Kildare. Clongowes, he wrote, was the best of the lot . . . 'They fed us well. They did not try to break your will and leave you spineless.'

He spent two years at the Royal University, the descendant of the Catholic University of Ireland which had been founded in 1854 by Cardinal John Henry Newman, but as over a period of six terms he managed to pass only two out of ten exams his mother transferred him to Trinity College. His love for Trinity emanates from every line he ever wrote about it. He loved the grey stone of the college quads, its crisp cut lawns and majestic campanile. Besides, 'Is there any college in the world that for its size has sent within the few centuries since it was founded more famous men near and far?' he once wrote. A keen

*Trinity College, Dublin (left)*
*The Queen Anne house at 15 Ely*
*Place (right)*

sportsman, he played cricket and soccer but cycling was his real love and much of his time at Trinity was spent pedalling around College Park, training for the many trophies he won. Socially he mixed less with the students and more with the dons, among them John Pentland Mahaffy, Henry Macran, Professor of Moral Philosophy, and Dr. Yelverton Tyrell, 'the wittiest man of his day and what a day it was'. With Tyrell he would sit having long philosophical discussions beneath the yew trees of Fairfield or in the doctor's Trinity rooms. Later he decided Grafton Street was one of the best streets in Dublin, partly because from it could be seen the great window wreathed in roses of sculptured stone of Professor Tyrell's spacious room.

During his college career he met James Joyce by chance and a friendship grew between them which would eventually lead to Gogarty being portrayed as Buck Mulligan in *Ulysses*. At one point they lived briefly together in the Martello Tower at Sandycove on the south side of the city, writing their verses on vellum sheets, sunbathing on the roof of the Tower, and entertaining friends at week-ends, including Arthur Griffith who later became the first head of the Irish Free State Government. In Gogarty's words, he and Joyce had their salad days together. Sadly as time went on their friendship ceased.

During his final year in medicine, in 1906, Gogarty married Martha Duane of Rossdhu near Moyard out in the wilds of Connemara in County Galway. She was the daughter of a landowning family that had been in the west of Ireland since at least the ninth century. Shortly afterwards he bought an old Queen Anne house with Gothic additions at 15 Ely Place, just off St. Stephen's Green. Though between 1915

69

and 1917 he rented it out and lived with his family in 32 St. Stephen's Green and at a cottage, once called Sea View and now renamed Capri, on Sorrento Road in Dalkey near Dublin, Ely Place was his home during his heyday in Ireland. From this house, now demolished to make way for the gallery of the Royal Hibernian Academy of Arts, Gogarty went to his work at the Meath and Richmond hospitals, gradually becoming a respected and successful ear, nose and throat specialist as well as a well-known man about town, his success being measured by the cars he drove, from an Argyll to a Daimler to a yellow Rolls Royce. Always full of energy, he often rode his horse out to Sandymount for a gallop on the strand or drove to Portmarnock beach for a run and a swim before breakfast. When he won his pilot's licence he would occasionally go out to Baldonnel airport for half an hour's flying.

Ely Place was always a hive of activity, with archery and tennis in the garden as well as outdoor theatricals. To Gogarty's Friday evening gatherings came Yeats, AE, James Stephens, Lennox Robinson, the tenor John McCormack and many others. During the War of Independence and the Civil War, Michael Collins frequently found shelter under Gogarty's sympathetic roof, for the writer had a great admiration for the Big Fellow. 'Napoleonic! But a bigger and a more comely specimen of manhood than Napoleon,' was how he once described him. When Collins was killed in 1922 in an ambush in County Cork it was a terrible blow for Gogarty. When the bloodstained key of Ely Place was found on his body, the writer called it a symbol of Ireland's shame.

Soon he had his own taste of the 'troubles' when, as a member of the Free State Senate, he was kidnapped one night from Ely Place by the Republican side. At the time his family was away at Mount Henry, a large country house they occasionally visited in the Killenard townland around Portarlington in County Laois. Gogarty, alone in Ely Place, was dawdling the evening away in the bath when he looked up to see a gunman in the room. He was held captive in a house on the banks of the river Liffey, near a salmon pool in the Islandbridge area. Later he outwitted his captors by leaping into the river and swimming to freedom. In thanks he presented two swans to the river, commemorating the occasion in his famous collection of poems, *An Offering of Swans.*

Though Gogarty escaped with his life, some of his property suffered.

*Kylemore House
(left)
Derryclare Lake,
Connemara
(right)*

Renvyle House, the old house formerly owned by the Blake family out beyond Tully Cross in Connemara which he had bought in 1917 as a holiday home, was burned down during the Civil War. While among the many treasures lost were letters from James Joyce and a magnificent library, Gogarty regretted one item above all the others: 'Of all I lost in Renvyle House I remember chiefly a self-portrait of my mother at sixteen, with her auburn hair divided in the middle, her plain blue dress, and an all-prevading air of sweetness and simplicity. No compensation can restore that.' When he got compensation he rebuilt the place as an hotel, with a small cottage nearby, affectionately called the Duck House, for the family's personal use. They often stayed at another house on an eleven-acre island, Freilaun or Heather island, in the middle of nearby Tully Lake which Gogarty loved because there he found 'blessed silence'.

He loved this part of Connemara and described it on more than one occasion as being coloured in so many hues that it was impossible to describe it in a language that had only about a dozen names for colour. Most of all he loved it for its location 'on the edge of the sea on the last shelf of Europe in the next parish to New York'. Another time he wrote: 'Were it not for the clouds off the Atlantic that break in rain, I would never leave Renvyle with its glimmering islands and its assured faith in wonders of the deep.' Though Renvyle was later sold, it still operates as an hotel.

There are two other houses in Galway associated with Gogarty, Kylemore House on the shores of Kylemore Lake which they owned and in which the family often stayed, and Dunguaire Castle, a

sixteenth-century tower house complete with bawn on the edge of Kinvara Bay. Built on the site of the ancient royal seat of a seventh-century king of Connaught, Guaire Aidhneach, the tower passed into the ownership in the seventeenth century of the Martyn family, one of whose descendants was Edward Martyn of Tulira Castle. Though Gogarty's son, Oliver, says his father bought Dunguaire because he always wanted to buy what he saw and liked, it has also been suggested that he acquired it to save it from demolition. Some years after the family ceased to own it the castle was renovated and it is now open to visitors.

In 1937 Gogarty was involved in a bitter libel action. A Dublin man, Henry Morris Sinclair, sued him on the grounds that certain allegations in the memoirs, *As I Was Going Down Sackville Street*, referred to him. The case attracted widespread publicity and Gogarty lost. Costs and damages amounted to about £2,000, and shortly afterwards he decided to leave Ireland and make himself a new life in America.

When he came home on visits he stayed either with his son Oliver at 22 Earlsfort Terrace, or around the corner at a small hotel, the Hatch Hotel, in Hatch Street. By 1957 he was planning to return home permanently but that same year he died at the Beth David Hospital in New York, after having a heart attack on the street. He was flown home and buried in Ballynakill cemetery between Moyard and Cleggan in the heart of the Connemara he had loved so well.

# Lady Augusta Gregory

## 1852-1932

The avenue of ilex trees still stands at Coole near Gort in County Galway and the great copper beech in the garden, autographed over the years by the legendary leaders of the Irish literary renaissance. But the great house itself is gone, pulled down within ten years of the death of its most famous occupant, Lady Gregory. Perhaps its angriest epitaph came from Seán O'Casey: 'All the rooms and passages are gone, and saplings root among the broken stone, for an elevated Irish Government has broken down the house and levelled it smooth for nettles to grow upon a shapeless mound. Oh! A scurvy act for an Irish Government to do on the memory of one who was greater than the whole bunch of them put together. . . .'

The lady O'Casey referred to had been born in the previous century, in 1852. Her name was Isabella Augusta and she was the twelfth child and youngest daughter of Dudley Persse whose ancestors, a branch of the Percy family from Northumberland, had, according to family tradition, come into Ireland in Cromwellian times. Altogether her father had sixteen children by two marriages. His bride each time was from the O'Grady family, the first being the Honorable Katharine O'Grady, the second her cousin, Frances Barry, daughter of Colonel Richard Barry of the now demolished Castle Cor in Kanturk in County Cork. She was Augusta's mother and through this side of the family the future playwright acquired as kinsman Standish Hayes O'Grady, the Irish scholar and translator.

At one time Dudley Persse owned nearly four thousand acres in County Galway around the family seat, Roxborough House, a white gabled eighteenth-century building with red blinds on its windows and

*The dining room,*
*Roxborough*
*House*

green-painted flower boxes on its sills. To one side flowed a stream which had been widened to make a lake in front of the house, and there was a three-acre garden with strawberries growing along its paths, and pears, cherries and peaches covering its walls. In those days Roxborough was like a small mediaeval enclave. Within its confines were a smithy, sawmill, coach house, dairy, laundry, carpenter's workshop and kennels, with a yard in the middle where all the activities went on. Here and there throughout the estate the Atlantic could be glimpsed from the ruined towers that remained from an earlier age.

Making life even more exciting for the child Augusta at Roxborough was the presence of her dashing brothers, particularly Dudley who was said to have killed seven Russians during the Crimean war, at the battle of the Alma. He brought many memories back to County Galway, and once when a younger brother played on the piano, *Partant pour La Syrie*, a tune used by the French army of the day as its battle hymn, he became very moved and gave the child a sovereign. Though never perhaps as fine a rider as her brothers, Augusta had her own pony, Shamrock, on which she roamed the demesne, and in summer the young people would go to Chevy Chase, a shooting lodge on a hill near the main house which was adorned with stags' heads, horns, and bundles of heather from the wild countryside outside. There as a child she played at being housekeeper for the others.

Educated at home, the boys by a tutor, the girls by a governess, the biggest single influence on Augusta's early life was probably that of her Irish-speaking nurse, Mary Sheridan, among whose memories were the cries of the rebels when the French, coming to assist them in rebellion against the English, landed in Killala in 1798. Into her small charge, Mary instilled an interest in Irish history which prompted her to buy Fenian pamphlets when on visits to the nearby town of Loughrea, paying for them with the sixpences she earned for reciting faultlessly from the Bible. All this was unusual in a house rooted in the Ascendency tradition which W. B. Yeats summed up thus: 'They had all the necessities of life on the mountain, or within the walls of their demesne, exporting great quantities of game, ruling their tenants as had their fathers before, with a despotic benevolence, were admired and perhaps loved, for the Irish people, however lawless, respect a rule founded upon some visible supremacy.'

This, however, seems to have been an over-romantic interpretation of the Persses' status in the community. The fact remains that at the end of the eighteenth century Roxborough had been attacked by one of the secret group of rebels bent on redressing land grievances, and later Augusta's father narrowly missed being assassinated by a Fenian sniper; the fact that his wife worked as a proselytizer among her Catholic servants and tenantry cannot have added to the family's popularity. Though by the time of the Civil War, 1922–1923, the then master of Roxborough, Augusta's nephew Arthur, was a better liked landlord than any Persse for generations, the house was still destroyed. Occupied by members of the Republican side, who left it unguarded when they had finished their business, it is thought to have been looted and set fire to by marauders. Revisiting it after the event, Augusta found it strange to see the homestead that had sheltered them all, a deserted, disconsolate ruin, 'all silent that had been so full of life and stir in my childhood and never deserted until now'. Arthur Persse and his family moved to England. Today all that remains of Roxborough, at the end of the overgrown avenue, is the shell of the house just visible under a mass of ivy.

At the time of the fire Augusta had long left Roxborough. Though her elder sisters had been given a season at the Viceregal Court in Dublin, Elizabeth marrying Shawe Taylor of the now demolished Castle Taylor at Ardrahan in County Galway, and Adelaide marrying, against the family's wishes, a poor clergyman named Lane, Augusta does not seem to have been 'brought out' in this way, possibly because such a season was considered too expensive. She was not, however, without at least one suitor; a friend of her brother Frank's who was

sent packing by Mrs. Persse because she didn't consider him suitable.

Hopes of marrying her off must have all but faded when, at the age of twenty-eight, in Nice where she had gone with her mother in a vain attempt to nurse her brother Richard back to health, she met Sir William Gregory. Though he was aged sixty-three, a widower with no children, he was considered eligible and a few months later they were married at St. Matthais Church in Hatch Street in Dublin, the bride wearing grey rather than the traditional white, something she afterwards regretted. The following year a son, Robert, was born in London.

The Gregorys were descendants of a landed Warwickshire family, some of whom had settled in Ireland around the time of Cromwell. The family were well liked in Galway. Sir William's father had died of fever after ministering to his tenants during the famine years, while he himself, as a Member of Parliament, supported Catholic Emanicipation and worked to improve the lot of the Irish tenant farmer. As a former Governor of Ceylon, he brought his new wife to foreign places she might otherwise never have seen and introduced her to a new intellectual world. But without doubt the greatest thing he gave her was Coole Park, the home his great-grandfather, a wealthy East Indian Nabob, built near Gort about 1770. Though Sir William died only twelve years after his second marriage, Coole remained Lady Gregory's home for well over half a century.

'Although this house of Coole, that has been my home for half a hundred years, lies but seven miles from the home of my childhood, Roxborough, the estate being separated indeed at one point but by a field or two from the high demesne walls within which my childhood was passed, there had ever seemed to be a strangeness and romance about Coole,' she later wrote. According to one of her protégés, Seán O'Casey, who often visited her there, her two great loves were books and trees, and there was no shortage of either at Coole. Even in bad weather she would be out in her old black dress, black straw hat and galoshes, tearing back the ivy, nettles and thistles that clustered around the saplings, and tarring the barks of the bigger trees to ward off the rabbits. Of the woods she wrote: 'These woods have been well loved, well tended by some who came before me, and my affection has been no less than theirs. The generations of trees have been in my care, my comforters. Their companionship has often brought me peace.'

*Coole Park, left and overleaf*

*Duras
House,
Kinvara*

Though in Coole, at Inchy Wood, there were junipers and elsewhere rare conifers planted by her husband, perhaps the most unusual trees on the estate were the enormous catalpas. Brought to the demesne by some long gone Gregory, they had made their journey half-way across the world wrapped up in a cloth and carried by a servant. Years later George Moore would infuriate Lady Gregory by mistaking one of them for a weeping ash.

As her interest in literature grew, she was by no means isolated from kindred spirits in the west of Ireland. She visited often with the playwright Edward Martyn, a member of one of the country's rare Catholic landed families, at Tulira Castle, near Ardrahan in County Galway, the old tower house that he had added to and Gothicized to please the mother who dominated him. Another of her favourite haunts was Duras House, just beyond Kinvara, also in County Galway, on the edge of the Burren and close to the sea. Now a youth hostel, it was then the home of one Count Florimond de Basterot, a French litterateur who spent part of each year there. 'In his garden, under his friendly eye, the Irish National Theatre, though not under that name, was born,' wrote W. B. Yeats later in his memoirs, of the foundation of the theatre we know today as the Abbey.

Over the following twenty years Yeats was to spend virtually every summer at Coole in a room specially reserved for him in the centre of the house and above the library, from which he had a view of the lake on the estate. Looking back, he wrote: 'In later years I was to know the edges of that lake better than any spot on earth, to know it in all the changes of the seasons, to find there always some new beauty.' Years

82

were to pass, he wrote, before he came to understand the later eighteenth and early nineteenth century and to love that house more than all other houses. In his poetry he was to immortalize it all, particularly the swans. Lady Gregory did everything to facilitate him at Coole, regularly leaving out clean pens, fresh ink and a spotless blotter on the desk where he wrote in the drawing-room. In this same room, with its red and poppy patterned Morris wallpaper, she herself wrote almost all her plays and books, sitting at the great Empire desk which her husband had used before her, the centre drawer of which fascinated her grandchhildren because of its 'ever growing, ever vanishing collection of pencils, paintbrushes, penknives, tools, scissors and the like'. Strewn here and there on the floor were boxes filled with letters she had received over the years from such great names as Thomas Hardy, Henry James, Mark Twain and Augustus John.

When she was in her sixties, two great blows befell Lady Gregory. The first was the drowning, in the torpedoed *Lusitania*, of her beloved nephew, Hugh Lane, but the second struck even harder for that was the death of her son Robert, her only child, killed in action in 1918 somewhere over the Austrian lines in Italy. Though even this did not defeat her, she wrote at the time that her heart was very sore for the fair-haired son who had been so gentle and affectionate to her throughout all his life. Her great consolation were the three children he left behind him, Richard, Anne and Catherine, the 'chicks' as Lady Gregory called them, all of whom had been born at Coole and in her book, *Me and Nu: Childhood at Coole,* Anne Gregory has given us an enchanting picture of what life was like for them in those days. In the summer there would be afternoon tea outside, on the gravel sweep by the front door, and when it was colder the children would sit around in front of the library fire, being read to by Grandma, a fir-cone or a handful of kippeens being thrown into the hearth occasionally to get a real blaze going. The high point of the year was always Christmas when after dinner on the day itself the children would be ushered into the breakfast-room to see the huge tree all ablaze with candles, with mountains of presents gathered underneath waiting to be unwrapped.

During those years the great passion of Lady Gregory's life was to keep Coole in the family. Unlike many other big houses it survived the 'troubles', mainly because of the respect for the family in the locality. 'Tell her Ladyship that we wouldn't hurt a hair of anyone in her

Ladyship's family,' a band of armed men told her granddaughters once when they encountered them in the Nut Wood near the house. Coole, however, was never legally hers, having passed on the death of her son to his widow. In the late 1920s it was sold to the Land Commission, but a proviso was included whereby she could stay on as a tenant, on the payment of £100 a year.

'As I sit here in the wintertime or rough autumn weather, I sometimes hear the call of wild geese and see them flying high in the air, towards the sea. I have gone far out in the world, east and west in my time, and so the peace within these enclosing walls is fitting for the evening of my days,' she wrote. Towards the end she had herself helped on a final journey through all Coole's rooms so she might see for the last time the things she had lived with for the best part of her life, most of all the books: 'I shall be sorry to leave all these volumes among which I have lived. They have felt the pressure of my fingers. They have been my friends.'

Lady Gregory died in 1932 and she was buried in the Protestant plot of the new cemetery in Galway, beside her sister, Mrs. Arabella Waithman of Merlin Park. In a prophetic poem, *Coole Park 1929*, Yeats had written.

> *Here, traveller, scholar, poet, take your stand*
> *When all those rooms and passages are gone,*
> *When nettles wave upon a shapeless mound*
> *And saplings root among the broken stone*

Within ten years of her death, Coole Park had been demolished. The knocker of its front door was presented as a keepsake to the Abbey Theatre's green-room, a brass door knob given as a memento to George Bernard Shaw.

Lady Gregory's worst premonitions had come true. Years before she had written that Coole was both a home of culture and a place of peace which, if dismantled and left to ruin, would be the whole of Ireland's loss: 'I think the country would be poorer without Coole.'

# James Joyce

## 1882-1941

James Joyce lived the greater part of his life outside Dublin; but in his imagination he never left it. On page after page of his writings the city is there, and no man could have mapped it better for as a boy he had been given a unique chance to see most parts at first hand – by belonging to a family that seemed to be perpetually on the move. By the time he was twenty, they had changed house at least fourteen times, the only trouble being that, as his brother Stanislaus later put it, each move represented a descending step on the ladder of their fortunes.

Their father John Joyce, known as Pappie, was a drinking man whose way of life would eventually drag the family down, but things were probably bright enough when James, his first child to survive, was born in the pleasant south-side suburb of Rathgar, at 41 Brighton Square West, a two-storey red brick terraced house, looking out over the triangular shaped park in the centre of the square. Shortly after his birth they moved to 23 Castlewood Avenue in nearby Rathmines, but Pappie had a hankering to live by the sea and also wanted to live beyond the reach of his wife's relatives, so in 1887 he moved the family to a fine house in the seaside resort of Bray in County Wicklow, a few miles south of the city. The address was 1 Martello Terrace, and from its windows the children had an excellent view of the Esplanade and could watch the sea when, on a wild day, it crashed over the wall to swirl about in the street below.

In Bray Pappie had a chance to indulge in the sporting life, rowing stroke of a four-oared boat at the Bray Regatta, swimming, and fishing for plaice and flounders. On Sundays friends would come out for the day from Dublin, and to Mrs. Joyce's accompaniment on the piano,

*23 Castlewood Avenue (left)*
*1 Martello Terrace (right)*
*23 Carysfort Avenue (far right)*

there would be singing in the drawing-room. When James was six he sang with his parents at a function in Bray Boat Club. There were now numerous children in the family who regularly staged nursery theatricals and indulged in what Stanislaus called 'bloodless clashes' with some urchins who lived close by. During the day James attended Miss Raynor's kindergarten with little Eileen Vance who, like so many of the people he knew, would later turn up in his writing. As a child he hated thunderstorms, locking himself into a cupboard in terror while they lasted.

It was while the Joyces lived in Bray that they were joined by Mrs. Herne Conway from Cork who became the children's governess and who was known as Dante, thought by Stanislaus to be a mispronunciation of Auntie. To Pappie she was, however, always known as 'that old bitch upstairs'. A fervent believer, Mrs. Conway would lead the family in the Rosary and the Litany of the Blessed Virgin, and occasionally took the children on religious pilgrimages, once to see the crib at Inchicore, another time to the National Gallery to see the picture depicting the Last Day. In those years the part played by the Catholic church in bringing about Parnell's downfall was hotly discussed. Dante took the Church side which led to disagreements with Mr. Joyce, culminating in the famous row during the Christmas dinner later re called in *A Portrait of the Artist*.

At the age of six and a half, his belongings packed into a trunk engraved with his initials, JAJ, James was sent to Clongowes Wood College, one of the most prestigious Catholic boarding-schools in the country. It was run by the Jesuits, in the magnificent setting of the

former Castle Browne, near Sallins in County Kildare.

In 1892 the family moved back into Dublin, to the suburb of Blackrock where they lived at 23 Carysfort Avenue in a house called Leoville. Here James spent much of his time studying at a leather-covered desk in the corner of the dining-room, for by now he had been taken away from Clongowes. Pappie, an employee in the office of the Collector of Rates, had been pensioned off at the age of forty-two and from then on the family's fortunes truly began to decline. Though he owned some property in Cork he eventually mortgaged it out of his possession, and the odd jobs he got such as advertisement canvasser for *The Freeman's Journal* or assisting in a solicitor's office never paid enough.

When they moved again some months later, across the river Liffey to the north side of the city, it was to what would be the last of their good addresses, 14 Fitzgibbon Street, off Mountjoy Square, a once elegant area most of which has since been demolished. From here the boys went to the Christian Brothers school on North Richmond Street off the North Circular Road, a move none of them relished. Oliver St. John Gogarty's father may have thought the Brothers the best educators in Ireland, but Mr. Joyce did not concur. He thought them plodders and much preferred the Jesuits, so it must have been with alacrity that he accepted an offer from a Jesuit acquaintance, Father John Conmee, to take his sons into Belvedere College free of charge. The College in Great Denmark Street, on the other side of Mountjoy Square, was built in 1775 for George Rochford, the second Earl of Belvedere and had magnificent stucco work by Michael Stapleton.

Meanwhile as bills accumulated and with landlords pressing Pappie for rent, the pace of the family's house removals accelerated. They moved first to 29 Hardwicke Street, behind Belvedere, now given over to Corporation blocks of flats, then to Millbourne Avenue in the north-side suburb of Drumcondra, which Stanislaus liked because being close to hills, woods and the river Tolka it was like living in the country. The neighbours, however, were not so charming. They worked mainly as navvies and farm-hands and lived in delapidated cottages; their children, one with the evocative name of Pisser Duffy, taking pleasure in hurling stones at the Joyce children and calling them names. One sad night, however, when Mr. Joyce in a drunken fit tried to kill his wife the neighbours must have felt that at last the family had sunk to their own level, for when they were on the move again Pisser's father called to the house to convey the good wishes of the cottagers.

Their next house was 17 North Richmond Street, a three-storey Georgian house with a basement, across the street from their old Christian Brothers school. From this house, when he was sober, Pappie would occasionally take his brood on strolls through the city, pointing out to them now and then places associated with such figures as Swift, Addison and Surgeon Wilde, father of Oscar. As he grew older, James began to explore Dublin by himself and in time made his way to Monto, the notorious red light district. This area of brothels, centred around Mecklenburg Street which later became Tyrone Street and then Railway Street, was totally wiped out around 1925, but it is remembered through Joyce who christened it Nighttown after a

*Millbourne Avenue (far left)*
*17 North Richmond Street*
*(centre left)*
*2 Belvedere Place (near left)*
*29 Windsor Terrace (right)*
*Richmond Avenue (far right):*
*No. 13 no longer exists*

term picked up from his journalist friends who used it to describe the late-night shift in their offices.

On a more respectable level James also frequently visited the homes of his school friends, particularly that of the Sheehy family at 2 Belvedere Place, off Mountjoy Square. At the Sunday evening gatherings here he would join in charades, sing old favourites like *The Croppy Boy* and *Take a Pair of Sparkling Eyes,* and dance with the youngest daughter of the house, Mary Sheehy, for whom he harboured a secret passion for years. Later she married his friend, the poet Tom Kettle, who was killed in action during the first World War.

It was at the first Joyce home in the north-side district of Fairview, 29 Windsor Avenue, that James's love of Ibsen began. Here he sat up all night to read *The Master Builder* which he had ordered by post. This interest continued when the family moved to 7 Convent Avenue and 13 Richmond Avenue, two other streets in Fairview, unfortunately much altered over the years. It was to the last address that Ibsen sent an indirect message of thanks to the young man who had written an article about him in *The Fortnightly Review.* When it arrived, James, who was out skylarking with one of the girls on the avenue, was overwhelmed. He replied: 'Dear Sir, I wish to thank you for your kindness in writing to me. I am a young Irishman, eighteen years old, and the words of Ibsen I shall keep in my heart all my life.' When he went to University College, he made it his mission to educate his fellow-students about Ibsen. Again he wrote to the playwright: 'I have sounded your name defiantly through the college where it was either unknown or known faintly and darkly.'

The last of their Fairview addresses was 8 Royal Terrace, and it was here that James finalized his first play, *A Brilliant Career,* which he later destroyed. Soon the family was on the move again. By now, moving had developed into a routine. Some of the family went early in the day, the rest following later in the evening, behind the float which carried their continually dwindling belongings. Alongside walked Pappie, singing a love song. He had at this stage devised a series of stratagems to avoid having to pay the rent, including one whereby he agreed to leave voluntarily, thus sparing the landlord the legal costs of getting them evicted, on condition that he was given a receipt as a reference to enable him to rent quarters elsewhere.

The next house, 32 Glengariff Parade, off the North Circular Road, was to be a sad address for the family. There Georgie, known to his father as 'the nipper', died as a result of typhoid fever which had been carelessly treated. During Georgie's last illness his father would read to him and James would sing his adaptation of *Who goes with Fergus?* When he died, Belvedere, where he had been a favourite pupil, organized the funeral. Everyone was deeply upset; even one of the Jesuits who had called to offer condolences wept when he saw the little boy's body. Though Mrs. Joyce apparently thought James was unmoved by the death, Stanislaus remembered how his brother had crept up the stairs into the bedroom and sat looking at the body of his young brother before it was taken away. When his own son was born years later, he was given the name Giorgio.

Meanwhile he was making a name for himself as a writer in University College, through the Literary and Historical Society, and

*8 Royal Terrace, now*
*8 Inverness Road (far left)*
*32 Glengariff Parade (left)*
*7 St. Peter's Terrace (right)*

had come to know Yeats and other figures of the Irish literary renaissance. Later he decided to go to Paris to study medicine, a slightly bizarre decision which was doomed to failure.

While away he wrote home often and his mother did her best to respond, throwing some light on their relationship. 'My dear Jim,' she wrote, 'If you are disappointed in my letter and if as usual I fail to understand what you wish to explain, believe me it is not from any want of a longing desire to do so and speak the words you want but as you so often said I am stupid and cannot grasp the great thoughts which are yours much as I desire to do so. Do not wear your soul out with tears but be as usually brave and look hopefully to the future.' After a brief visit home for Christmas, he went back to Paris but soon sensed something was wrong. On 10 April 1903, he wrote: 'Dear Mother. Please write to me at once if you can and tell me what is wrong.' Next day the answer came in a telegram, not from her but from Pappie. 'Mother dying come home Father ' it read, and having borrowed the money he set out.

By this time, Pappie, by cutting his pension in half, had finally bought a house off the Cabra Road in Phibsboro at 7 St. Peter's Terrace, now part of St. Peter's Road, which Stanislaus called Bleak House. There, not long after her eldest son's return, May Joyce died of cancer at the age of forty-four. Her family clustered, grief-stricken, around her bedside. Though Stanislaus, who hated his father, denounced Pappie's whining after her death as hypocrisy, he had undoubtedly loved her in his own way. Mabel, the baby of the family, was inconsolable in her sorrow and it was James who sat up on the

stairs late into the night with his arms around her, trying to ease the pain.

If things had been difficult before Mrs. Joyce's death, they became disastrous afterwards, with the furniture being pawned or sold and mortgages taken out on the house until they lost it altogether. Through all these disturbances, James wrote the first draft of what became *Stephen Hero* and ultimately *A Portrait of the Artist*.

On 10 June 1904 he first met Nora Barnacle, the woman with whom he was to live out his life. Tall and auburn-haired she was striding confidently along Nassau Street; when he spoke to her she did not rebuff him. She was then a young girl from Galway working as a chambermaid in Finn's Hotel at 1–2 Leinster Street, the name of which though faded is still visible on the red brick gable wall of the building that faces towards Trinity College Park. Four days later, however, she failed to turn up for their first rendezvous and Joyce wrote: 'I may be blind. I looked for a long while at a head of reddish-brown hair and decided it was not yours. I went home quite dejected. I would like to make an appointment but it might not suit you. I hope you will be kind enough to make one with me – if you have not forgotton me.'

So it was on 16 June that they first went out walking together. Later he was to immortalize the day by making it that on which the action of *Ulysses* took place, and ever since it has been known as Bloomsday.

Around this time he finally moved away from home and rented a room at 60 Shelbourne Road, Ballsbridge. There, on a hired piano, he rehearsed for the tenor competition in the Feis Cheoil, won the year before by John McCormack. Here too he wrote the first stories for what

*60 Shelbourne Road (far left)
Joyce stayed briefly at No. 103
(left) and No. 35 Strand Road,
Sandymount (right)*

eventually became *Dubliners*. Later he spent some weeks living with his friend Oliver St. John Gogarty in the Martello Tower by the sea at Sandycove, near the famous men-only bathing place, the Forty-Foot. The tower, which was one of a series of defences built by the British during Napoleonic times in case of French invasion, stands forty feet high, with walls eight feet thick; the rent was £8 a year. Today it is preserved as a Joyce museum and is filled with memorabilia connected with the author.

When Joyce finally decided to leave Ireland, in 1904, he took Nora with him. Neither completely trusted the other. When passing through London he left her alone in a park for a few hours and she thought he might not come back. He did, however, and as his biographer Richard Ellmann has written: 'He was to surprise his friends, and perhaps himself too, by his future constancy. As for Nora, she was steadfast for the rest of her life.'

After that departure he was to make three visits home. The first was in 1909 when he stayed with his family at 44 Fontenoy Street, a road off Mountjoy Street near the city centre. There, softened by the sight of his little grandson, Giorgio, Pappie who had been hostile when James left Ireland with Nora made peace with his eldest son, taking him for a walk in the country and singing for him an aria from *Traviata*. James also made a pilgrimage to Galway to see the house on Augustine Street where Nora had lived with her grandmother. When he visited Nora's mother at 4 Bowling Green, Mrs. Barnacle sang for him *The Lass of Aughrim*.

Having discovered that there was no regular cinema in Dublin, and

95

*44 Fontenoy Street*
*Merrion strand from Strand*
*Road ( below )*

that money could be made by establishing one, Joyce persuaded some businessmen in Trieste to invest money in the project. He returned to Ireland that same year and set up The Volta cinema at 45 Mary Street in the centre of town. Unfortunately the venture failed but the visit home did give him the chance to slip into Finn's Hotel and see the room that had once been Nora's: 'I have been in the room where she passed so often, with a strange dream of love in her young heart. My God, my eyes are full of tears...' he wrote of this experience. But his letters to her in Trieste betrayed no love of his native city. In one he says: 'How sick, sick, sick I am of Dublin! It is the city of failure, of rancour and of unhappiness. I long to be out of it.'

In 1912, with Nora and their two children, he spent much of the summer in Ireland, particularly at Bowling Green from where he visited Oughterard to see the grave of Nora's old sweetheart, Michael Bodkin. But his disillusionment with Ireland was complete when the publishing firm of Maunsel scrapped plans, at the eleventh hour, to bring out *Dubliners*. He would never come home again. When he died abroad, in 1941, he was buried in Zurich. Nora, who died ten years later, is buried in the same cemetery.

96

# Francis Ledwidge

## 1887-1917

Of all the men who went to their deaths on the western front in the first World War, none carried with him a greater love of home than Francis Ledwidge, and the home that he thought of was Slane in County Meath.

Whenever he was away, all his dreams kept calling him back there. Writing once to a friend, Lizzie Healy, from a camp near Basingstoke he expressed how he felt: 'I feel sure that I will return again safely and then, and then! Yes, when the war is over, if I am not shot, I am coming back to Slane. I love it very much because from nowhere else have I ever had such calls to my heart. I love Stanley Hill and all the distances so blue around it. I love the Boyne and the fields through which it sings. I love the peace of it above all.' Before him then were the horrors of Gallipoli, hardship in Siberia and hospitalization in Cairo, but the vision of Slane never left him.

In a letter from France to the writer Katharine Tynan he wrote of how he heard the roads calling, and the hills and the rivers, wondering where he was. It was terrible, he added, to be always homesick. 'You are in Meath now, I suppose,' he wrote to her another time. 'If you go to Tara, go to Rath-na-Ri and look all around you from the hills of Drumconrath in the north to the plains of Enfield in the south, where Allen Bog begins, and remember me to every hill and wood and ruin, for my heart is there. If it is a clear day you will see Slane blue and distant. Say I will come back again surely, and maybe you will hear pipes in the grass or a fairy horn and the hounds of Finn – I have heard them often from Tara.'

A few weeks later he was dead, his body blown to bits by a German

shell as, with some other soldiers, he was building a road on the outskirts of Ypres near the Belgium village of Boesinghe. His remains
were buried close by, in what they call the Artillery Wood cemetery.

Though Ledwidge's memories of Slane encompassed the whole
magnificent area, his own home was actually a very small and in-
significant part of it, one of two local authority cottages at Janeville
just outside the town. It was in this small house of kitchen, living-room
and three bedrooms that the eight surviving Ledwidge children grew
up. While Francis was still only a child, their father died unexpectedly.
Though he had only been a farm labourer they were now bereft of even
that small income, and worried that she might become totally destitute
relatives and friends urged Mrs. Ledwidge to put the younger children
into care. Instead she determined to keep them all together, by
working in the fields of neighbours, taking in their washing and
mending their clothes. So poor was the family that when the eldest son.
Patrick, died of tuberculosis, the parish had to provide his coffin.

In spite of poverty and tragedy, however, Ledwidge's childhood was
a happy one. With his brother Joe he fished the river Boyne for perch
and eel, played football in the shed field and had fun when the monthly
cattle market was held on the fair green. Together the pair attended
the local school where the master, Mr. Madden, though often
frustrated by the gifted Francis also recognised his genius. Once years
later, on reading a poem by his former pupil in the local newspaper,
*The Drogheda Independent,* he remarked to the somewhat astonished
clientele in a Slane pub, 'I taught that boy.' From an early age
Ledwidge wrote poems and saved his pennies to buy anything from
*The Arabian Nights* to the poems of Keats and Longfellow, and this interest continued when he left school at the age of thirteen to become a
farmer's boy. When inspiration suddenly took hold of him in the fields,
he scribbled the verse down on a gate-post or a cow shed; on whatever
happened to be handy.

Though his working life was not to last long it was certainly varied.
After work in the fields he got a job as a houseboy in the local mansion,
Slane Castle, seat of the Marquis of Conyngham. Later he went to
work in Drogheda, a few miles away, for a grocer, baker and public
house owner named Larry Carpenter. From there his mother moved
him to Rathfarnham, a suburb of Dublin city, to work at the grocery
establishment of one W. T. Daly. However, loneliness for his beloved

*Ledwidge's cottage, and view of Slane*

Slane overcame him and after only a few days in the place he crept out one night when the whole house was sleeping and walked the thirty odd miles home. From then on all his jobs were in Meath. After a period as a gardener in Newgrange and a stint back in the fields, he worked on the roads, and later got a job in a copper mine in Beauparc, from which he was fired for trying to improve conditions for his workmates.

He went back to road labouring and was made a foreman, cycling wide tracts of the county to oversee the work, living at the old barracks in Martry, between Kells and Navan. All this time he was writing, spurred on by the encouragement he got from his fellow Meathman, Lord Dunsany, who was also a writer. Ledwidge had sent him some of his poems and Dunsany had written back a letter hailing him as a true poet. In the years that followed he became Francis's friend and patron, studying his work, lending him books from the library at Dunsany Castle and even, for a time, giving him an allowance. 'All things that were swift in their coming, and brief, remind me of Ledwidge,' wrote Dunsany who thought of him as the poet of the blackbird, born to be the singer of the hills and fields of Meath.

Meanwhile, Ledwidge had fallen in love with Ellie Vaughey, a young Slane girl. When she worked as a milliner in Drogheda, living in the nearby seaside village of Mornington, he would walk with her on the shore. But his happiness was not to last. Though by now he had an indoor job as secretary to the Meath Labour Union, it was only temporary. Ellie's family owned half the hill of Slane, so her marriage with a man of such uncertain means as Ledwidge was out of the question.

*Slane Castle (left)*
*View from the*
*hill of Slane (right)*

When she married another man it broke his heart and though subsequently he asked Lizzie Healy, another local girl, to wait for him until the war was over he never forgot Ellie. When she died in childbirth in Manchester in 1915, he was among the group who brought her on her last sad journey back to Slane.

By then he had already joined the Royal Inniskilling Fusiliers, a move that seems strange for such a home-lover but one that was possibly precipitated by the loss of Ellie. Another consideration could have been the lack of secure employment at home. He himself gave another reason. He was a member of the Navan Rural District Council and Board of Guardians and he listened to the frequent debates on the war with feelings of impatience: 'I joined the British Army because she stood between Ireland and an enemy common to our civilization and I would not have her say that she defended us while we did nothing at home but pass resolutions.'

Sadly he lived to have second thoughts about his decision. Once when home on leave, he told his brother Joe that even if the Germans were walking up the garden path he would not join up again, but then it was too late. By the end of the summer of 1917 he was dead.

> *He shall not hear the bittern cry*
> *In the wild sky, where he is lain,*
> *Nor voices of the sweeter birds*
> *Above the wailing of the rain*

# Charles Lever

## 1806-1872

So happy was the Dublin home into which the novelist Charles Lever was born that it was called Sunnybank. The house, which no longer exists, was in Amiens Street, then called the North Strand, a few hundred yards from the centre-city landmark of Nelson Pillar. By all accounts it was a most hospitable place where guests got plenty to eat and had an entertaining time. His mother was an Irishwoman, born Julia Candler, and she married James Lever, an Englishman of old Lancashire stock, who worked in Dublin as a builder on such important constructions as the Custom House and the General Post Office.

As a boy at Sunnybank, young Charley had a small theatre out at the back where he dabbled with paints, made stage scenery and occasionally put on plays with his little friend, Sophia Louche, for an audience that often consisted only of the cook or perhaps one of Mr. Lever's apprentices. Years later Sophia would remember him as a chap who didn't eat meat and who spent his pocket money on books. She also thought him an expert mimic and a capital singer of songs; most of all he impressed her, a little later in life, as a boy who would 'never make love to any girl whom he did not mean to make his wife'. He was a frequent visitor to some cousins in the County Kilkenny village of Inistioge on the river Nore, where he produced such plays as *Bombastes Furioso* and *The Warwickshire Wag*, and fell in love with the countryside, particularly the demesne of the now ruined Woodstock House with its magnificent beechwoods. While staying in Inistioge he must have heard many stories about the Fownes and Tighes, the owners of Woodstock; a relative of the Fownes was one of the famous 'Ladies of Llangollen' in Wales. He later delineated the neighbour-

102

*Nelson's Pillar and O'Connell Street*

103

hood in such works as *The Daltons* and *Lord Kilgobbin*.

In Dublin he attended many schools including one run by a dreaded Mr. Ford, notorious for his terrible thrashings, another at 56 William Street run by Mr. Florence McCarthy, and a third at 113 Abbey Street under Mr. William O'Callaghan. But most of his schooldays were spent at Wright's Academy, 2 Great Denmark Street, under the charge of a certain Reverend George Newenham Wright who was very strict. Here, Lever was remembered as a boy who preferred to have his head buried in romances than in lexicons or grammers, as a fascinating story-teller and an agile fencer and dancer. Nearby, in Grenville Street, there was another boys' school of a somewhat inferior status and the two sets of pupils were constantly fighting. During one pitched battle, in Mountjoy Fields, Reverend Wright's boys went so far as to use home-made explosives, an offence for which they landed themselves before the law at Marlborough Street police station. However, the versatile Charley extricated them from this predicament, putting in such an elequent defence on his own behalf and that of his fellow culprits that he managed to get them all off with only a few fines to pay.

In his leisure time he would wander along the quays looking through the book barrows for a bargain, or watching for a glimpse of Miss Kate Baker, the young lady with whom he fell in love and who later became his wife; she lived with her family at Sir John Rogerson's Quay.

When Lever entered Trinity College he had rooms on the ground floor of No. 2 Botany Bay, one of the residential squares in the College. He also lived at Lisle House, 33 Molesworth Street, a fashionable

*The gardens at Woodstock (left) Burgh Quay and the Custom House in 1820 (right)*

boarding-house of the period. When he obtained his BA, he went on to study medicine, attending classes at Sir Patrick Dun's Hospital and Dr. Steeven's Hospital. Later he recalled one unusual dissection during which the corpse gave his dissectors a shock by sitting up, waving his arms about and shrieking aloud.

An inveterate traveller throughout his life, he visited America as a young man and spent some time with an Indian tribe. When he returned he gave his full attention to building up his practice as a doctor. He lived for a time at Moatfield, the house his father built in the Dublin suburb of Clontarf, and for a longer period at the family's next home, 74 Talbot Street in the centre city. During the cholera epidemic of 1832 he worked in County Clare, at Kilrush and Kilkee, before becoming a dispensary doctor in Portstewart, County Derry, a fashionable watering-place. Here he wrote some of the novel *Harry Lorrequer*. Around this time he married Kate Baker and the couple started their life together at Verandah Cottage in Portstewart. By now his practice extended to the towns of Portrush, Coleraine and Derry, his dashing personality earning him such nicknames as Dr. Quicksilver and The Mad Doctor.

After a time working as a doctor in Belgium, Lever returned to Dublin, living briefly in the suburbs of Stillorgan and Glenageary before finding the mansion at Templeogue that is the home most associated with him. A former domain of the Knights Templars, the house was built over an old subterranean passage with an ancient wattle and clay roof, and is one of the houses at which King James II is said to have stayed at on the night of his defeat at the Battle of the

Boyne. Lever called it his 'Chateau de Templeogue' and the place, in those days, lived up to the title, having within its demesne an old Dutch waterfall, a series of garden grottos, extensive courtyards enclosed by high walls and massive gate piers. Here, along its sweeping paths and long avenue, the novelist rode with Julia, Charley junior and Pussy, the three children a friend once called his leverets. And in the hospitable style he had learned from his parents he entertained his friends, Thackeray and Isaac Butt, the leader of the Irish Parliamentary Party in the English House of Commons, being but two of the notables who made their way out to Templeogue. When some time later Thackeray's *Irish Sketch Book* appeared, it contained a special dedication to Charles Lever, 'a friend from whom I have received a hundred acts of kindness and cordial hospitality'; at Templeogue, he added, one could find not only wax candles but also some of the best wine in Europe. So good were the whist parties held there that they often lasted all day and night and attracted so many guests that once all the wheels of their carriages became entangled in the avenue, locked so fast that help had to be sought to free them. In the middle of it all, according to one friend, 'no one shone with greater lustre than the host himself'.

When not entertaining he would work in his 'snuggery', the walls of which were lined with book shelves and carvings, and where art objects, manuscripts and issues of *The Dublin University Magazine*, which he edited, were usually strewn on the floor. Here he would write beneath the red glow of a carcel lamp, undisturbed except by Kiffer, his German factotum, bringing him his coffee and curaçao or summoning him out to dinner.

Later, after a brief stay in a house called Oatlands in Stillorgan, Lever again left Ireland to live on the continent. For a time he was British Consul in Trieste. However, it was on his frequent visits to Ireland that, in his own words, he was at his happiest. The best houses were open to him, and he would socialize again with the men who when they were younger had been members of a club founded by Lever, called the Burschenschaft, where German was spoken, much wine consumed and where wit was the order of the day. So keen was the repartee at one of these reunion dinners that the waiters had to try and hide their laughter behind napkins. Of one visit home, in 1865, he wrote: 'I never experience the same lightness of heart, the same

*Lever's 'Chateau de Templeogue'*

capacity for enjoyment, the same readiness to employ whatever faculties I possess as in Ireland; and as I walked through the old courts of Trinity, I felt a thrill through me as though thirty hard years of struggle and conflict were no more than a troubled ocean, and that there I stood, as ready for heaven knows what fun or frolic, of freshman's folly and hot youth's wild gaiety, as when I lived yonder, over there at No. 2 chambers with Frank——, my chum, and the junior Dean over my head.' He told his friend, John Pentland Mahaffy, that he had to come home now and then to have his mind refreshed by nights in Trinity, among friends, hearing again all the local news and listening to the music of the Irish brogue.

As the old friends died off, however, the visits grew sadder. 'A sort of lurking fear oppresses me,' he wrote after a visit to Trinity, 'that I am looking at that old college park for the last time.' In fact this was not his last visit. He came back once more, before returning to Trieste where he died in 1872. He is buried there in the English cemetery. Of him when he lay dead, a friend wrote: 'He was still lying as in sleep, with his coat and vest off. Only for the shadow of death upon his calm countenance, it was hard to believe that he had gone from amongst us. He had as all bear testimony who knew him intimately a wonderful power of attaching you to him, and winning, not merely liking, but actual love and affection.'

107

# George Moore

## 1852-1933

George Moore may have spent the most exciting years of his life in Paris and London but he was born and lived his early life in one of the remotest parts of the west of Ireland, County Mayo, where the Moores had lived for at least six generations before him.

The Moores claimed descent from Sir Thomas More, Lord Chancellor of England under Henry VIII and author of *Utopia,* and the family settled first at Ashbrook House near Ballyvary, later moving to the environs of Ballyglass. Here, at the close of the eighteenth century, the writer's great-grandfather, another George Moore, built himself a Georgian mansion with the fortune he had amassed in the Spanish town of Alicante. 'I have travelled far but have seen nothing as beautiful as Lough Carra,' he declared when installed in Moore Hall, a fine three-storied house with a basement below and an immense circular gravel sweep in front of the main door. Inside, the hall had an Adam ceiling and contained a huge iron chest, supposed by successive generations of Moore children to be filled with Spanish gold. Overhead was the summer room with a balcony looking out over the lake. As with all great houses of the time, Moore Hall had a chapel, greenhouses, bakery, laundry, blacksmith's forge and extensive servants' quarters.

In this house the writer George Moore had a happy childhood. With his three brothers and sister he listened with rapt attention while his mother recited by heart from the novels of Walter Scott and to the tales his father told of a journey he had made to the east as a young man. Upstairs, in a closet in George's nursery, were kept the swords, scimitars, daggers and Arab bridles from that journey, which

*Lough Carra,*
*County Mayo (left)*
*Moore Hall from*
*an old print (right)*

fascinated him all through his early life.

As a boy George's best friend was his younger brother, Maurice, though he occasionally played with Oscar and Willie Wilde who spent several childhood summers at Cong, also in County Mayo. Another character who figured in his youth was his grandmother, Louisa Browne, the granddaughter of the first Earl of Altamont of Westport House, County Mayo, who, as an old invalided lady, would be carried by two nurses into the gardens at Moore Hall if the day was fine. When she died, young George remembered how his father sat by the bed on which her body lay, trying to write letters but weeping bitterly.

When the time came to go to school, he was sent to England, to Oscott, where his standards unfortunately were not always up to those of his father. Occasionally there were threats that the young scholar might not be allowed home to Mayo for holidays, which led to heart-broken pleas for leniency. 'If you will take me home for the vacation, I will try to improve myself. If you only know what I will suffer by stopping here . . . for goodness' sake take me home,' pleaded the little boy in a letter, and apparently his appeal did prevail in the end. Later, however, ill-health necessitated a more lasting stay at home. 'Those two years spent at Moore Hall were the best part of my childhood,' he recalled, 'Long days spent on the lake, two boatmen rowing us from island to island, fishing for trout and eels. How delightful!' Much time was also spent at his father's racing stables where the boy's ponies, Spark and Twinkle, were stabled alongside champions like Corunna, Anonymous and Croaghpatrick, the winner of the Stewards' Cup at Goodwood.

110

The idyll ended some years later. His father, having regained a seat in Parliament, moved the family to London to be near Westminster, but while on a business visit home to Mayo he died, the victim of a sudden attack of apoplexy. When Mrs. Moore travelled over for the funeral, George came with her, not only as a mourner but as the heir to his father's estates, comprising 12,371 acres in Mayo and 110 acres in neighbouring County Roscommon, worth in rents about £4,000 a year. No doubt the tenants looked at him curiously, wondering what kind of a landlord he would make, but he already knew that this was one role he would not fill. He wanted to be an artist and soon afterwards he went off to Paris, taking with him a young boy from Moore Hall, William Moloney, to act as manservant. Writing back to Joe Aplely, the butler at the Hall, William told of how hard his young master worked, starting at eight every morning and continuing until five in the evenings: 'Mr. George is as happy as a prince here, and not a foolish hare in his body but so good-natured a person never lived.' He would, William added, become a great artist.

Later George turned to writing instead and settled in London, his affairs in Mayo being handled first by his uncle, Joe Blake of Ballinafad, and later by an agent, Tom Ruttledge. When George visited, he would spend all day writing, going out at dusk to walk the land in slightly unsuitable leggings – blue silk stockings set off by black patent shoes. To the astonishment of the locals he would occasionally pretend he had forgotten his English and could speak only in French. It was on visits to Moore Hall that much of *A Mummer's Wife* was written. In the early 1880s, he spent part of the winter in Dublin, at

111

·the Shelbourne Hotel, attending the levees, castle balls and other functions of the social season, observing first-hand a world he would later reproduce in *A Drama in Muslin*. As time passed, however, it was his brother Maurice, with his wife and two sons, who maintained the family presence at Moore Hall.

About the beginning of the century, George Moore returned to live in Ireland, not at Moore Hall but in Dublin. The reasons for his return are not exactly clear. It could have beeen horror at the Boer War, though he himself told his friends later that one day, while walking down a London street, he heard a mysterious voice telling him to leave England and return to Ireland, to herald a Celtic revival. Certainly he had acquired a renewed enthusiasm for his native land, particularly its language which he valued to such an extent that he threatened to disinherit Maurice's sons unless they learned it.

In Dublin he had trouble finding a suitable house, in spite of numerous searches made with the aid of a jarvey. In his mind he had an exact impression of what he wanted: 'My imagination turned rather to a quiet old-fashioned house with a garden, situated in some sequestered half-forgotten street in which old ladies live – pious women who would pass my window every Sunday, along the pavement on their way to church.' In the end, the writer George Russell, AE, found for Moore what he described as the perfect residence for a man of letters. The house, No. 4 Upper Ely Place, was one of five little eighteenth-century dwellings in a quiet cul-de-sac which was at that time cut off from the main thoroughfare by tall iron gates. Ely Place and nearby Hume Street had been developed as the result of a marriage between the Ely and Hume families in 1736, the centre-piece of the complex being Ely House, originally occupied by members of that family. The rent of Moore's more modest house was £100 a year, with a bit extra for the use of a nearby orchard. The writer who thought of the place as The Garden of Eden – Paradise on earth – instantly agreed to take it, sending over to London for such treasured possessions as his Aubusson carpet and his Impressionist paintings. When he moved in, he found to his delight that the house looked out over a convent grounds, Loreto Convent in St. Stephen's Green. There on fine days, he had a bird's eye view of the nuns' underwear out drying on a line.

What he probably liked best about the house was the garden, even if

*The Shelbourne Hotel, and reception room at Dublin Castle.*                    113

he was convinced that some of its most delicate plants had been killed off by fumes from the College of Surgeons on the far side of St. Stephen's Green, Here during the summer, meals would be served *al fresco* to Moore and his guests, sometimes including Oliver St. John Gogarty who also lived in Ely Place. Sadly, Moore's relations with his other neighbours were not so cordial. Until he took up residence, all the hall doors in his part of the street had been painted white and residents were outraged when he had his repainted in a brilliant green. A lawsuit was threatened. The writer retaliated by rattling his stick on the railings each night, to waken all the neighbourhood dogs. The residents counter-attacked by hiring an organ-grinder to play in the street outside, just as Moore was sitting down to write. However, in spite of distractions, he worked away, on *The Lake, The Untilled Field*, and parts of his three-volume autobiography, *Hail and Farewell*.

From Ely Place, Moore watched the gradual decay of the area, the worst blow being when a shop opened in his beloved St. Stephen's Green: 'I cried, other shops will follow and this beautiful city of Dublin will become in a very few years as garish as London.' To keep the country's capital city as lovely as it was, it might, he thought, be almost worth letting it slumber on in its Catholicism, the religion he detested and which he formally abandoned, causing a rift to grow between himself and Maurice, which, coupled with other disagreements, led to Maurice leaving Moore Hall in 1911. The great mansion was closed up, never again to be reopened.

By then George, disenchanted with Dublin, had returned to London. He is said to have reached his decision while staying with the Leslies at Glaslough in County Monaghan. There, on an island in the lake, he saw a signpost, erected by one of the children as a joke, with the words 'London 398 miles' written on it. This he took to be an omen, as mysterious as the voice that had called him back to Ireland many years before, and so he left: 'On a grey windless morning in February the train took me to Kingstown, and I had always looked forward to leaving Ireland in May, seeking the words of a last farewell or murmuring the words of Catullus when he journeyed over land and sea to burn the body of his brother, fitting them to my circumstance by the change of a single word: *Atque in Perpetuum, Mater, Ave Atque Vale.*' It was a cold bleak morning and, travelling on a sea without a ripple, he went below to think of the friends he had left behind him, feeling

*The ruins of Moore Hall (right and overleaf)*

himself to be only a humble fellow.

He did, however, come over again on visits. During the Civil War, 1922–1923, he had nightmares about Moore Hall being burned. His brother was now a Free State Senator and George knew that he and anything connected with him could be a target for the Republican side. On 1 February 1923, the dreaded news came in the form of a telegram from the family's steward, James Reilly. It read: 'Moore Hall burned down last night, nothing saved.' In a following letter, Reilly told Maurice that there was absolutely nothing left but the walls of the house. Recounting how he had tried to dissuade the raiders, he went on to describe the fire: 'At five am I ventured out, it was then pitch dark and pouring rain, imagine my horror, when I got to the hill overlooking the garden and saw the whole house one seething mass of flames, huge tongues of fire were, shooting out of every door and window, clouds of sparks like snow-flakes were being carried away by the wind which was south-west. I at once knew there was no hope, even if I had help nothing could be done . . . .' He felt, he said, as he stood by, like one would feel standing by the open grave of a very dear friend ' . . . At six o'clock the roof went in with one huge crash and there was nothing left only smouldering ruins of my favourite charge on which I had spent twelve years' jealous care. It sickens me when I think of it all.'

George received £7,000 compensation but he did not rebuild Moore Hall. He sold it and the remaining land to the State. Later Maurice bought back some of the land, including the ruin, hoping that he might one day restore it, but this never happened. Though George left a

fortune of £80,000 when he died in 1933, it went to other relatives; Maurice, with whom no reconciliation had ever been achieved, was cut out completely. Nevertheless it was Maurice, once his dearest friend, who carried out his brother's unorthodox wishes about his burial. George Moore was cremated in London, and Maurice had a vase copied from a bronze-age urn in the museum in Dublin and had a hollow carved out to hold it on Castle Island in Lough Carra where they had both so often played as boys. There, the May after his death, a small group of friends accompanied his ashes on their last journey home.

Maurice is buried not far away in the family's burial ground in Kiltoom woods with many of his ancestors. Though all their names are listed on the tombstones, for their epitaph the visitor must look at the inscription by the wall on the road outside, erected in the family's honour, perhaps in recompense. 'Burial place of the Moores of Moore Hall,' it reads, 'This Catholic patriot family is honoured for their famine relief and their refusal to barter principles for English gold. Erected by Ballyglass Coy. old IRA 1964.'

Further along the road and up through the trees, the Hall still stands looking, in certain lights and at a distance, as beautiful as it must have been in its heyday.

# Seán O'Casey

## 1880-1964

Although Seán O'Casey was not born into a Dublin tenement, his plays were inspired by the Dublin he knew as a child, a city riddled with poverty and decay. By the time he came into the world, in 1880, his mother had already seen the majority of her children out of it. Yet the playwright never regretted his early circumstances and later wrote that all his life he carried with him both the wisdom and the courage that exposure to those conditions had given him.

The family name was Casey, and as they were Protestants in a predominantly Catholic country Mr. Casey took his religion seriously. With his clerical abilities he could probably have got himself a better-paid job; instead he worked for most of his life with a proselytizing organization in Townsend Street, the Irish Church Mission, supplementing his income by acting as caretaker at No. 85 Upper Dorset Street, now demolished. There his youngest son Seán, initially called John, was born, not far from the house which had seen the birth, one hundred and thirty years before, of another famous dramatist, Richard Brinsley Sheridan.

Within a year or two the Caseys had moved to 9 Innisfallen Parade, a quiet road off Dorset Street which Sean later remembered as the place where he really started life. There he probably slept in the front room with brothers Tom, Mick and Archie, going to class each day, from the age of five, to St. Mary's Infant School on Lower Dominick Street where his sister Bella was the principal teacher. From an early age he suffered from a chronic eye disease which meant regular trips to the hospital and constant help with his homework from Bella and Mrs. Casey. Each night they coached him, making him learn by heart tracts

from his text-books and from the Bible, so that when the inspector came to the school he could give the impression of being able to read.

When his father died, in his late forties, the family was left without a breadwinner, and Mrs. Casey took young Johnny to live with his sister in the two-roomed attic flat above the school in Lower Dominick Street. He now attended St. Mary's National School, and when the family again moved house he was enrolled at St. Barnabas National School where later his class-mates remembered the bandages that often covered his sore eyes.

The Casey's new home was in a different part of the city, in Hawthorne Terrace, behind the North Wall near Dublin Bay. The number is uncertain. Some say it was 22, others 25, and the suggestion has also been made that they lived in both houses at different times. In Hawthorne Terrace a piano had been left behind by a former tenant and Archie, who had a theatrical bent, constructed a makeshift stage where he and his brothers and the children of various neighbours often put on plays. Even the dog took part. Though Johnny left school at the age of fourteen to start the first of a series of jobs, from stockboy and sweeper to navvy on the railway, he never lost his early interest in drama and often played with the Townsend Street dramatic group. Once when a stand-in was needed at the Old Mechanics Theatre in Abbey Street the future playwright filled the breach by playing Father Dolan in *The Shaughraun* by Dublin-born Dion Boucicault. Years later the same theatre would be rebuilt as the Abbey, with which O'Casey's career was to be so closely linked.

As a young man he was interested in everything going on around

*Plaque on O'Casey's birthplace at 85 Dorset Street (far left)*
*9 Innisfallen Parade (left)*
*Hawthorne Terrace (right)*

him. He learned Irish, called himself Seán O Cathasaigh, and joined the Gaelic League. He also took up the pipes and was a founder member of the St. Laurence O'Toole Pipers Band. Any money he had to spare went on the books he found in the barrows outside bookshops on the city quays. At 18 Abercorn Road, where the family lived since 1897, his nieces and nephews were warned, when they came on visits, not to disturb their uncle if he was reading.

He was becoming more and more aware of the appalling conditions in which the majority of Dubliners lived, and when labour leader Jim Larkin came to the city to try and improve things Seán enthusiastically joined his Irish Transport and General Workers' Union and took an active part in the general strike and the lock-out that followed in 1913 and lasted for eight months. When the Citizen Army was formed to protect the striking workers and their families during this bitter, sometimes violent, confrontation with the employers of Dublin, O'Casey was a part of it. Though he did not get involved in the Easter Rebellion of 1916, his name as an activist was known to the authorities and he was rounded up with other suspects and kept overnight in St. Barnabas Church. Later they were moved to a cellar nearby where they passed the time playing cards and listening to the chat of the soldiers. Echoes of those days are heard every time *The Plough and the Stars* is played.

When his mother died in 1918, Seán lived on with his brother Mick at Abercorn Road. Mick was the character of the family, able to sign his name with both hands simultaneously. He was also a hard drinker; once when a jug of stout fell to the floor, smashing into smithereens, he

*18 Abercorn Road (left)*
*422 North Circular Road ,*
*where O'Casey's early plays*
*were written (right)*

is said to have got down on all fours to lap up its contents. After their mother died, however, the brothers fought. The rows were sometimes so loud they kept the neighbours awake at night, and finally the pair split up. When Seán left Ireland their contact with one another was sporadic, but years later Mick is said to have read *Autobiography* and commented that, when all was said and done, you had to hand it to him.

After leaving Mick, O'Casey moved to 35 Mountjoy Square, now demolished, where he shared quarters with an Irish-speaking Aran islander, Michael O Maolain, who remembered how Seán sang in a soft tenor voice, a voice that reminded him of the song of the robin. He later moved to 422 North Circular Road where he lived and wrote in the same room, a habit that to some extent he retained all his life. At the age of forty-four he had given up the hard life of a manual worker and decided to try and live by writing alone. It was in the house in North Circular Road that his great early plays were written. He sent them to the Abbey which soon recognized his genius.

With success came heartache and, like Synge before him, O'Casey's work was to be decried by many of his countrymen. When on 8 February 1926, *The Plough and the Stars* was produced, it incensed Irish nationalists. O'Casey brought the Republican flag into a pub which was sacrilege; he portrayed an Irish girl as a prostitute, and his sympathies were plainly with the women and children of the country, rather than with those out fighting for its freedom. The audiences didn't like it. At the fourth performance, vegetables, shoes and chairs were hurled on to the stage. In the balcony hecklers drowned out the

voices of the cast by singing *The Soldiers' Song*, and finally one group leaped up on to the stage and started to assault the actors. The curtain was dropped, the police called and the crowd dispersed, but not before Yeats declared that O'Casey's fame had been born there that night; that the cradle of genius had been rocked by the Dublin people who had disgraced themselves yet again.

That night was a turning point in O'Casey's life. Describing it in the third person in his *Autobiography*, he wrote: 'For the first time in his life, Seán left a surge of hatred for Cathleen ni Houlihan sweeping over him. He saw now that the one who had the walk of a queen could be a bitch at times. She galled the hearts of her children who dared to be above the ordinary, and she often slew her best ones. She had hounded Parnell to death; she had yelled and torn at Yeats, at Synge, and now she was doing the same to him.'

Strapping his belongings into a suitcase he took a jaunting-car to the train and was soon on the mail-boat, 'feeling her sway and shyly throb beneath his feet; watching the landing-stage drift far away, getting his last glimpse of Eireann – separated for the first time from her, and never likely to stand settled on her soil again.' In 1928, his controversial war play, *The Silver Tassie,* was rejected by the Abbey and the severance was complete.

Meanwhile in England he had met the Dublin-born actress, Eileen Reynolds Carey, and they married on 23 September 1927. They had three children; Breon, Shivaun and Niall, who died of leukaemia when he was twenty. To his wife, just before he died in Torquay in Devon where he had settled, O'Casey wrote: 'You are and have been indeed, Cuisle Mo Chroidhe, the pulse of my heart; and this heart of mine loves you and will love you unto the last. Oh, my darling girl . . .'

Though he visited Ireland over the years and his plays have never ceased to be performed, that departure in 1926 was the end of an era, as well he knew when recalling it afterwards: 'The ship turned giddily to right, to left, plunged with upturned bows, dipping them again as quick, for there was more than a half-gale blowing. Seán had been anxious about sea-sickness, but he felt no discomfort. He was a good sailor. He faced resolutely towards where the ship was going. Sweet Inishfallen, fare thee well! For ever!'

# George Bernard Shaw

## 1856-1950

As a boy and a young man, George Bernard Shaw was not over-enamoured with his native city of Dublin, possibly because of the unsettled household into which he was born. Though his father, George Carr Shaw, came from a well-off and socially prominent family which had come to Ireland at the close of the seventeenth century and had, over two centuries, produced bankers, clergymen, stockbrokers, civil servants, even a baronet, he unfortunately belonged to a poorer branch. Pensioned off from a job at the Four Courts, he bought his own wholesale corn business but it did not prosper, and this coupled with his drinking problem further depleted the family fortunes. When he was over forty he married Elizabeth Gurly, a young woman from a reasonably affluent family, but the tyrannical aunt who reared her cut her out of her will. GBS later commented on the end result of it all: 'We were finally dropped socially. After my early childhood I cannot remember ever paying a visit to a relative's house. If my mother and father had dined out, or gone to a party, their children would have been much more astonished than if the house had caught fire.'

By his own account, the house where he was born, 3 Upper Synge Street, now No. 33, a two-storey Georgian terraced house over a basement, was a dismal place. Meals were eaten in the kitchen and too often the children were served overstewed beef, badly cooked potatoes and tea left so long on the hob that it had turned to pure tannin. Young George, variously called Bob, Sonny, Ginger, Copperhead and other names when he was small, later felt that as a child no one had particularly cared for him. He remembered neither love, hate, fear nor reverence within his childhood home.

*33 Synge Street
( far left)
1 Hatch Street
( left)
St. Stephen's Green
( right)*

His mother hadn't much time for him, with the result that he idolized her. It was a rare and delightful occasion when she deigned to butter the bread for him in her own inimitable thick and uneven way, while to be allowed to accompany her on a walk, visit or excursion was considered a remarkable privilege. Mostly his days were spent in the company of servant girls and nurses, one of whom had instructions to air young Shaw on the banks of the canal or around the fashionable squares 'where the atmosphere was esteemed salubrious and the sur-roundings gentlemanly'. What actually happened, however, was that she took him to visit her private friends in the slums; whenever she met a generous male acquaintance who insisted on treating her, she took young George into the public house bar where he was given lemonade and ginger beer. He did not relish these trips as, like many a drinking man, Mr. Shaw had instilled into his son the belief that all bars were wicked places.

The young writer's formal education began with a governess, Miss Caroline Hill, who baffled him with her attempts to teach him to read, for by then he had already mastered the art himself. 'I can remember no time at which a page of print was not intelligible to me, and can only suppose that I was born literate,' he said later. In time, however, he did acknowledge that Miss Hill must have taught him something by instructing his bankers to make an annual subscription to The Governesses' Benevolent Institution. His next teacher was a clerical uncle, the Reverend William George Carroll, who taught him a great deal of Latin – all of which he claimed he forgot after a few years.

The first school he attended was the Wesleyan Connexional where

he didn't exactly wear himself out working: 'I never did any "prep" at home for the Wesleyan, being an incorrigibly lazy shirk at that age, and a shameless liar in making "excuses".' After a short period at school in Glasthule, he was sent to the Central Model School in Marlborough Street, which must have been a humiliating experience for him, the son of a Protestant and a gentleman, for here most of the boys were Catholics from the lower middle classes. Later he attended the Dublin Scientific and Commercial Day School in Aungier Street.

To Shaw, however, time spent in such institutions was akin to time spent in jail and all his real learning was done at home, largely under the influence of a dynamic individual named George John Vandaleur Lee. This man, a musician who taught singing by a new method, was the teacher of Mrs. Shaw who possessed a fine mezzo-soprano voice. Under his guidance she excelled and sang under the name of Hilda at the Antient Concert Rooms in Brunswick Street. Already unhappy in her marriage, from this point on she became more and more involved in the world of music.

Eventually she became Lee's assistant and the Shaws went to live with him at No. 1 Hatch Street, a much finer and larger Georgian house off Leeson Street, only a few yards away from St. Stephen's Green in the heart of the city. 'The arrangement was economical,' wrote Shaw, somewhat wryly, of the slightly unorthodox arrangement, 'for we could not afford to live in a fashionable house and Lee could not afford to live in an unfashionable one, though being a bachelor he needed only a music room and a bedroom.' Young George was soon able to whistle at will from the works of Verdi, Gounod, Handel and

*Torca Cottage, Dalkey (left) View of Dublin bay from Torca (right)*

others, including Mozart who was his favourite. Lee was not the only musical influence in his life, for his father played the trombone, occasionally entertaining the public at out-of-doors concerts on summer evenings. In the Shaw family there had been a tradition of ophicleide, violin, cello, harp and tambourine players, and at the headquarters of the clan in the Bushy Park area of the city musical evenings were not uncommon. Unfortunately, George Carr Shaw and his brood were rarely invited.

To round out his extracurricular education young Shaw also paid regular visits to the Queens Theatre and to the Royal where he was entranced by the performance of the actor Barry Sullivan who moved gracefully about the stage and whose voice carried to every corner of the theatre. Later Shaw also remembered the delight and astonishment he felt when the curtain went up on his first opera. In the afternoons the future playwright would wander through the frequently deserted room of the National Gallery; he acknowledged his debt to this institution by leaving it a handsome legacy. Later he was to enroll for classes at the Royal Academy of Art. He read extensively and played out various roles always preferring to be the villain; Mephistopheles had a special fascination for him.

Mr. Lee's influence on the Shaw family was not confined to musical matters. He was a health fanatic and as a result of his guidance GBS became an inveterate eater of brown bread and always slept with his window open at night. Lee insured that the family got plenty of air in the summer by buying and presenting to Mrs. Shaw a house high up off the Vico Road by the sea at Dalkey, a few miles outside Dublin city.

126

This was Torca Cottage where young George was very happy. He particularly loved the scenery: 'There is not two penn'orth of Alpine mountain or tree in that landscape; but I have never seen more beautiful skies, even in Venice; and I always look at the sky.'

When he left school, he got a job at Uniacke Townshend, a land agent's office in Molesworth Street; here he specialized in teaching operatic scores to the young fellows who worked with him. By this time, Mrs. Shaw, tired of her husband's inadequacies, had almost entirely taken over the running of her family's affairs, and when Lee moved to London in 1872 she decided that her best course of action was to follow him and continue her work there as a singing-teacher. Young George stayed in Ireland with his father, both of them moving into lodgings at 61 Harcourt Street, off St. Stephen's Green. But soon he, too, became disillusioned with his native city where all around him he saw failure and poverty, obscurity and contempt. He decided the time had come to leave: 'There was no Gaelic League in those days, nor any sense that Ireland had in herself the seed of culture. Every Irishman who felt that his business in life was on the higher planes of the cultural professions felt that he must have a metropolitan domicile and an international culture; that is, felt that his first business was to get out of Ireland. I had the same feeling ... I showed my own appreciation of my native land in the usual Irish way, by getting out of it as soon as I possibly could.'

As long as there were other places to live, he never intended to settle again in Ireland, and from henceforth his life would be centred in England. It was almost thirty years after he had taken the emigrant

127

ship, carpet-bag in hand, before he returned on the first of a series of visits with his wife, Charlotte, and her sister and husband. They stayed with the Payne-Townshends in County Cork and in hotels at Glengarriff, Parknasilla, and Muckross in Killarney where a photograph of GBS and Charlotte still hangs. Invariably the party visited Mitchelstown Castle which covered a greater area than did any other private house in Ireland. In her book, *Crowned Harp*, Nora Robertson gives a description of the 'King's' bedroom: 'My husband and I counted forty-one stairs to get to the first floor. The room was square and of such a size that on a misty night it was difficult to see across it. I have a recollection of a deep crimson flock wall paper with a velvety pile that had resisted deterioration for upwards of a century. The immense canopied four-poster was like a fortress, only gained by assault, crowning as it did, the summit of a raised platform. Nothing less than this royal apartment was considered suitable for dear Charlotte and the pleasant Mr. Shaw. . . .'

Synge Street must have seemed a long, long way away.

*Mitchelstown Castle*

128

# Edith Somerville and Martin Ross

### 1858-1949                    1862-1915

Literary collaborators, second cousins, close friends, and in their own way lovers, Edith Somerville and Violet Martin did not meet until they were in their twenties. Though both were great-granddaughters of the famous Lord Chief Justice, Charles Kendal Bushe, they were born far apart, Edith in Greece, Violet at her father's home, Ross House, near Oughterard in County Galway.

The Martins, one of the most prominent families in the west, came to Ireland in the twelfth century, at the time of the Norman invasion, in the retinue of the de Burgos. Initially entrenched in Galway city, by 1590 one of the Martins had acquired the estate at Ross and though, being both Royalist and Roman Catholic, they lost their holdings in the city during the Cromwellian period, they retained their lands beyond it. They were one of the fourteen great families that the Cromwellian soldiers called the 'tribes' of Galway.

At one point there were four family strongholds in the county, at Dangan, Ross, Birch Hall, and Ballinahinch where Mary Martin, granddaughter of one of the family's most benevolent members, nicknamed Humanity Dick, was once heiress to almost 200,000 acres. Called the princess of Connemara, her territory also included fifty miles of Atlantic coastline but all of this was lost after the famine of 1847–1848 during which her father, Thomas, died of typhus after visiting some of his stricken tenants in the workhouse. Like most of his family he was well loved and in spite of the hard times his people followed his funeral in a procession that took two hours alone to pass the gates of Ross on its way to Galway.

Naturally the famine was also felt at Ross, seat of the most senior

branch of the family which had become Protestant by marriage. There Violet's father and his wife, Anna Selina, set up a soup kitchen to which starving people came from miles around, often stumbling half-crazed into the yard or through the downstairs passages of the house. Already beyond hope when they arrived, many died at the gates of Ross and were buried where they had fallen.

All this was past history when Violet was born in June 1862. It was, her sister remembered, 'A time of roses, when Ross was at its best, with its delightful old-fashioned gardens fragrant with midsummer flowers, and its shady walks at their darkest and greenest.' However as the eleventh daughter in a family of fourteen her welcome was not too rapturous. 'I am glad the Misthress is well,' said old Thady Connor, the steward, 'but I am sorry for other news.'

The nursery was already so full that she passed into it almost unnoticed. She could read at a very early age and would creep away to the drawing-room to leaf through the books that were kept there, in particular an edition of Milton illustrated with terrifying pictures. The family soon had a nickname for her, 'The Little Philosopher.' Family life was happy at Ross. The days began with psalms and lesson readings. In the afternoons the children roamed the estate, sometimes staying indoors to stage theatricals under the supervision of their eldest brother Robert, the heir to Ross. One of his most memorable productions was an adaptation of *Bluebeard* in which he played the title role. The entire staff was commandeered as audience.

Ross was a beautiful spot in which to grow up. 'Bounded on the east by the long waters of Lough Corrib, on the west by the barren mountains stretching to the Atlantic, on the north by the great silences of Connemara,' Ross seemed, Violet later wrote, to be geographically intended for peace. The house, built in 1777 on the site of an older Martin castle, she thought of as a tall unlovely block of great solidity, with kitchen premises half underground, but still she loved it: 'It is said that a man is never in love till he is in love with a plain woman, and in spite of draughts, of exhausting flights of stairs, of chimneys that are the despair of sweeps, it has held the affection of five generations of Martins.'

Describing life at Ross she said it was of the traditional Irish kind, 'with many retainers at low wages, which works out as a costly establishment with nothing to show for it. A sheep a week and a cow a month were supplied by the farm, and assimilated by the household; it seemed as if with the farm produce, the abundance of dairy cows, the packed turf house, the fallen timber ready to be cut up, the fruitful garden, the game and the trout, there should have been affluence. But after all these followed the Saturday night labour bill.' During her father's lifetime Ross got into debt so that when he died in 1872 he left a far less prosperous estate than that which he himself had inherited. The whole order of life was changing too and before he died he saw his loyal tenants vote for a Home Rule candidate in the Parliamentary elections instead of the Conservative candidate who was his choice. Violet, always sensitive, understood that was going on: "With his death a curtain fell for ever on the old life at Ross, the stage darkened, and the keening of the tenants as they followed his coffin, a tremendous and sustained wail, like the voice of the grave itself, was the last music of the piece.'

When Robert inherited Ross he was in London working as a journalist and there he preferred to stay. Mindful that she had daughters to marry off, the widowed Mrs. Martin, always known as Mama, moved to Dublin. Ross was shut up. The door was barred and rabbits ran fearlessly up the broad limestone steps where the family had once sat talking on summer evenings. There the estate lay 'in the whispering stillness of its summer woods, and the monotony of its winter winds, producing heavy bags of woodcock after its kind while its master "shot folly as she flew" and found his game in the canards of Fleet Street and Westminster. It was inevitable as things stood,' wrote Violet, lamenting the fact that in that alienation both Ross and her brother were missing much that lay in the power of the one to give the other.

Inevitably things deteriorated while they were away. The agent left in charge embezzled the rents; the lessee at Ross let the house fall into disrepair. When, sixteen years later, Mama returned with two of her daughters, Selina and Violet, everything was changed. The drawing-room had been converted into a kitchen, the hothouse had become a sloping jungle of vines run wild; outside, the melon pit was filled with nettles and the stableyard so full of grass that it might as well have been a meadow. Desperately Violet tried to improve things. Day after day she weeded the flower beds, painted the doors in the house and cut back the laurels from the driveway. The tenants came to help with the restoration, working away for nothing but their dinners.

The family themselves tried to settle back into the old life and Violet records how, when a very active little old man broke into a dance in the hall, her mother responded with gusto: 'Mama, who was attired in a flowing pink dressing gown, and a black hat trimmed with lilac, became suddenly emulous, and, with her spade under her arm, joined in the jig. This lasted for about a minute, and was a never-to-be-forgotten sight. They skipped round the hall, they changed sides, they swept up to each other and back again, and finished with the deepest curtseys. . . .' Bonfires were still lit for returning members of the family but to Violet they seemed to be only attempts at recreating old times and as such both painful and wretched.

The spread of nationalism had broken the old bond between the gentry and the ordinary people and from now on things would never be quite the same again. 'There is a change and I can feel it,' she wrote at the time. Robert also felt it: 'He shot at Ross occasionally, he visited it now and then, and at every visit his perceptive nature was aware that a new spirit was abroad; in spite of the genuine and traditional feeling of the people for their old allies, in spite of their good breeding, and their anxious desire to conceal the rift. The separation had begun, and only those who have experienced it will understand how strange, how wounding it is.'

When in his late fifties, Robert returned to live permanently at Ross but he died a few months later. Shortly afterwards his mother moved out to live with a married daughter at her home, Waterfield, in Oughterard, leaving Ross to Robert's widow, Connie, and their daughter Barbara. In 1906, shortly after Mama's death, Violet, now known as Martin Ross, went to live at Castletownshend in County Cork, home of her cousin Edith Somerville. From then on she only returned to the west on visits. In 1914 Ross was sold, passing from the ownership of the Martin family to that of another prominent family, the Chavasses.

Edith Somerville was born in 1858 in Corfu, where her father was in command of the Third Buffs, and to her far-flung birthplace she owed her unusual second name of OEnone. Soon, however, her parents brought her home to Drishane, the Somerville family seat in Castletownshend, the Georgian house up above the Atlantic on the coast of West Cork where she was to live almost all her life through:

'Some impressions will hold their place in memory and for me among the most ineffaceable of these is the picture of what, as a child, I believed to be the most wonderful and splendid house in the world, my grandfather's old house, in which, after the patriarchal fashion of an older Ireland, my father and mother lived with him and my grandmother.'

Castletownshend was unusual for an Irish town of the time. Instead of containing just one big house it contained at least three: Drishane, home of the Somervilles; Glen Barrahane, the nineteenth-century seat of the Coghills; and Castle Townshend where the Townshends lived. To make it even cosier, intermarriage during the eighteenth and nineteenth century meant they were all related to one another. It was, in short, a nest of cousins and of landed gentry, a most civilized and homely place for growing families. Linking the houses together, Main Street fell 'unhesitatingly as Niagara' towards the sea below. Near the bottom were two sycamores, known locally as the Two Trees and accepted by all as the focal point of the town, which over the years has changed hardly at all.

When Edith, one of the seven surviving children of the marriage, was growing up she preferred to hang about the stables or wander with the dogs rather than spend long hours in the schoolroom with a governess. She also loved sketching and was later allowed to study art abroad, working under Colarossi and Delecluse in Paris. As a young woman she was introduced to Cork society at a debutantes' ball in Dunkathal House, Glanmire, where, very nervous, she clung to the arm of her subaltern brother Cameron, but though she participated in the usual

*Drishane (left)*
*St. Barrahane's*
*Church (right)*
*Castletownshend,*
*the village and*
*castle (overleaf)*

social occasions the idea of marriage did not appeal to her. When a favourite friend, Ethel Coghill, got married at St. Barrahane's Church in Castletownshend she was upset, and when the garlands went up through the town for her sister Hildegarde's marriage to her first cousin, Egerton Coghill, Edith spent the evening in her room weeping.

Mrs. Martin had taken Selina and Violet on a visit to Castletownshend where they stayed at Tally Ho and Mall Cottage in the village. When, in January 1886, Edith first met Violet at St. Barrahane's Church it was an immensely important encounter for both. Edith wrote: "It has proved the hinge of my life, the place where my fate, and hers, turned over, and new and unforeseen things began to happen to us.' After the two women became friendly Violet stayed more and more at Drishane, often sleeping the night there in Edith's room.

That friendship did not really take root until Edith returned from a trip to Paris. It was, she later recalled, one of those perfect summers that come sometimes to the south of Ireland. Tall delphiniums, Japanese iris, peonies and poppies filled the gardens that June, and often she and Martin would slip away to sit and talk on the warm short grass of the sheep fields around Drishane, listening to the cries of the curlews and seagulls and watching the white sails of the yachts out on the water below. In the afternoons there would be lawn tennis and tournaments in which the pair often partnered each other.

On those summer nights there would be choir practice or dancing and later some of the company might row out into the mouth of the harbour, to rock there gently in the moonlight until it was time to go

home. 'These are some of those Irish yesterdays, that came and went lightly, and were more memorable than Martin and I knew, that summer when first she came,' recalled Edith in her memoirs. Of their importance to one another she added: 'It was, as I have said, though then we knew it only dimly, the beginning for us, of a new era. For most boys and girls the varying, yet invariable, flirtations and emotional episodes of youth, are resolved and composed by marriage. To Martin and me was opened another way, and the flowering of both our lives was when we met each other.'

Almost from the start they began experimenting with creative writing, and although Violet was not always at Castletownshend the friendship continued. By 1887 they were working on a novel which the family called 'that nonsense of the girls' and which ultimately became *An Irish Cousin*. It was inspired by a visit to an old memory-filled Townshend house, Whitehall at Aghadown in County Cork, about thirteen miles from Drishane. As they were leaving in the evening, 'In the darkened facade of the long grey house, a window, just over the hall-door, caught our attention. In it, for an instant, was a white face. Trails of ivy hung over the panes, but we saw the face glimmer there for a minute and vanish.' Of the start of their career Edith said: 'Little as we may have achieved it, an ideal of Art rose then for us, far and faint as the half-moon, and often, like her, hidden in clouds, yet never quite lost or forgotten.'

When *An Irish Cousin* was published in 1889, the partnership that among other books was to produce *The Real Charlotte* and *Some Experiences of an Irish RM* was firmly established. While Edith occasion-

ally went to Ross, working there in Violet's bedroom, in front of a big
log fire, from the early 1890s on their life together was more and more
at Drishane. There, after the death of her mother, Edith became the
mistress of the house, ordering the stores, arranging the meals,
managing the servants and dealing with the rats that infested the
house. Even after her father's death, when Cameron inherited
Drishane, none of this changed. Under her influence, Drishane was a
matriarchy as it had been, by all accounts, in her mother's time.

Between writing, hunting, travelling and visiting with the family,
these were happy years; but they could not last for ever. Even before
the war of 1914–1918 omens of death were appearing. Edith saw the
*Titanic* as it passed within a few miles of Castletownshend on its first
and last voyage, 'racing to the west into the glow of a fierce winter
sunset.' Then after the war had begun, the *Lusitania* was torpedoed off
Galley Head, a few miles from Castletownshend. From the wreck
bodies floated up along the coast, their money and jewels often washed
in alongside them.

A more personal tragedy was soon to strike Edith. Martin fell ill and
had to be taken to the Glen Vera Hospital in Cork. She was suffering
from a brain tumour and though the prognosis was bleak, Edith sat
day by day at her bedside hoping for her recovery. To Cameron she
wrote that the best half of her life and soul were being torn away: 'No
one but she and I can know what we were to each other.' Martin died
just before Christmas in 1915 causing Edith to write: 'This black,
black year goes out in despair and tears.'

Others died then too. The war carried off some of the young men who had ridden out with the West Carbery hunt of which Edith was Master for many years. Of them she wrote: 'Gallant soldiers, dashing riders, dear boys; they have made the supreme sacrifice for their country, and they will ride no more with us. The hunt goes on; season follows season; the heather dies on the hills and the furze blossoms again in the spring. Other boys will come out to follow hounds, and learn those lessons that hunting best can teach, but there will never be better than those three: Ralph and Gerald Thornycroft and Harry Becher.'

Later, Edith lived through the Irish 'troubles' and she met Michael Collins, Commander-in-Chief of the Free State troops in the Civil War, only hours before he was killed. Though it was a harrowing time, with supplies hard to get, the roads unsafe and many big homes in the county burned down, the family's various homes in Castletownshend escaped. In 1936, however, long after the country was at peace again, Edith's beloved brother, Boyle, a retired Admiral of the British Navy, was shot at his home, The Point in Castletownshend; his murderers, it was said, left a note saying they chose Boyle because he was recruiting for the British navy by providing local boys with certificates of good character. Hearing of it in London, Edith and another brother, Jack, hurried home, to find Boyle's body still stretched on the floor in his hall, because the police would not let it be moved until their investigations were complete. The crime, for which no one was ever indicted, found little support in the country and was strongly denounced by the Prime Minister, Eamon de Valera.

Subsequently Edith, who had for many years been interested in spiritualism, began communicating, or so she believed, with the spirit of Boyle, just as she felt she had been doing for years with Martin. This explains why many of the books written after Martin's death still appeared in the joint names. Though Edith did live to have another deep relationship with a woman, this time the English composer Ethel Smyth who was later to fall in love with Virginia Woolf, ultimately Miss Smyth found Edith too virginal and fastidious and they never made a permanent life together.

In the years after Martin's death Edith became a horse-dealer, started one of the first Friesian herds in the country, and conquered the literary worlds of England and America. Though Martin had known the great names of the Irish literary revival, Edith lived to be

*Main Street, Castletownshend,
with the Two Trees*

honoured by them. At an Irish Academy of Letters dinner at Jammet's restaurant in Dublin she was placed between Yeats and AE, while her fellow county Corkmen, Frank O'Connor and Lennox Robinson, were present to toast her.

When she was eighty-eight, she had to leave Drishane, the house where she had lived almost all her life and over which she had presided for half a century. A nephew, Desmond Somerville, son of her brother Aylmer, inherited it and came to take up residence. With Hildegarde, now a widow, she went to live in the town at Tally Ho. It was an enormous upheaval but once ensconced with her nurse, four servants, a gardener and an odd-job man, she made the best of things. On her ninetieth birthday, forty congratulatory telegrams arrived and the BBC broadcast a tribute to her. Tears came into her eyes as she listened.

Finally, in 1949, she died and her coffin was carried by the local men down the steep hill in Castletownshend and up the steps to St. Barrahane's. She had come to join Martin in the graveyard at last. As she had written years before: 'Withered leaves, blowing in through the open window before a September gale, are falling on the page. Our summers are ended.'

# *John Millington Synge*

## *1871-1909*

It was a strange irony of fate that led John Millington Synge, born of ultraconservative Protestant and landowning stock, to find his inspiration in a primitive peasant and Catholic Ireland.

He was the son of John Hatch Synge, a barrister whose practice consisted mainly of conveyancing, and Kathleen Traill, the daughter of a staunchly Protestant family from County Antrim. For years, her father, the Reverend Robert Traill, was rector of Schull in County Cork but when he died of famine fever in 1847, his widow, who had a large family to rear, moved to 3 Orwell Park in Dublin.

John was the youngest and the fourth son of the five surviving children of John and Kathleen Synge, and he was born at 2 Newtown Villas, one of two semi-detached houses on the outskirts of the village of Rathfarnham, then in the heart of rich dairy farmland, looking out to the Dublin mountains.

Before young John was a year old his father died of smallpox and his widow moved to 4 Orwell Park, renting the house beside her mother. Another of the Traill family also lived close by, and a third who had married a Northern Ireland clergyman, William Steward Ross, often came to visit at No. 3 with her family. Young John grew up in an atmosphere prevaded by family and inevitably his mother and grandmother became dominating figures in his life.

In those days, Orwell Park consisted of only a few houses and a Presbyterian Manse. One of the chief local landmarks was an old mill in nearby Dartry Park, and there John used to play with Samuel, the brother nearest to him in age and with whom he shared a bedroom at the top rear of the house. John also spent much time roaming the

*4 Orwell Park*

*2 Newtown Villas where Synge*
*was born (left)*
*Crosthwaite Park West (right)*

demesne of Rathfarnham Castle, a sixteenth-century mansion which was for many years the home of the prominent Ely family, and later of the Right Hon. Francis Blackburne, Lord Chancellor of Ireland; it is now owned by the Jesuits. Here, through his ten shilling telescope, the young writer would observe the comings and goings of bird, squirrels and other animals, often in the company of his cousin Florence Ross who entered with fascination into the magical world of next door where her Synge cousins kept not only dogs and cats, but pigeons, rabbits and canaries as well. As a child John loved Florence dearly, treasuring each little note she wrote him and even occasionally kissing the chair where she had sat. Years later Synge remembered his childhood as happy, though the strong religious background, with its emphasis on Hell and damnation, terrified him at times.

From Orwell Park he travelled every day to Mr. Herrick's Classical and English School at 4 Upper Leeson Street, walking on fine days, taking the tram when it rained. Later he went to Aravon House, a school in Bray, going down the new Dartry Park Road to catch the train. In time the regular routine of school-going proved too much for his delicate health and he was kept at home. Three times a week a tutor called for classes and, when he was sixteen, a Mr. Griffith began coming to give him violin lessons.

Every summer, Mrs. Synge, a great believer in the beneficial results of a change of air, took the family to the seaside, chiefly to Greystones in County Wicklow, a small fishing village some miles beyond Bray. One factor which probably appealed to Mrs. Synge was the strongly Protestant character of Greystones which was the home of the La

142

Touche family, some members of which had been prominent in the evangelical movement, a tradition in which she herself had been raised. In all they spent sixteen summers there, staying at such houses, as Menlo, Prospect House, Westview, Trafalgar House, Bushfield House, and others on Stanley and Bethel Terrace, many of which have since had their names changed. Another was Rathdown House on the left hand side of the road from Bray just past the cemetery, which had spectacular views of the big and little Sugarloaf mountains that dominate the Wicklow landscape, as well as a panorama from the front rooms of the tiny harbour below and the boats pulled up on the shore. Recalling those years, Samuel wrote how each summer there fulfilled the expectations they had had all autumn, winter and spring: 'How we loved Greystones! Your uncle John and I could there pick flowers and berries in the country round, or play on the shore, or sail our numerous small boats in the pools on the rocks.' One summer they stayed at the nearby inland village of Delgany at a house called Dromont where tennis and cricket were played in the garden.

During those years Synge joined the Dublin Naturalists' Field Club, entered Trinity in 1888, and began to attend lectures at the Royal Academy of Music. It was at this stage that his mother and family began to worry about his future. He had, in his own words, relinquished the Kingdom of God , and begun to take a real interest in the kingdom of Ireland . And he talked of making music his career.

In 1890, Harry Stephens, the young solicitor who had married Synge's sister, decided to leave Orwell Park where they were living. His practice was expanding and he wanted, in the words of his son

*31 Crosthwaite Park*
*West (left)*
*Glanmore Castle,*
*Ashford (right)*

Edward, to move 'to some neighbourhood more fashionable than the quiet blind alley of Orwell Park'. His mother-in-law put it more diplomatically, saying that the move was not provoked by any dislike on Harry's part for Rathgar but that he wanted 'to be among people he can know and make friends of to further his business'. The place he chose was Kingstown, now Dun Laoghaire, a few miles south of the city, which had been opened up over sixty years before by the construction of the first railway in Ireland which linked it with Dublin. It was also the packet-station for England, and gradually became an important and attractive seaside suburb for a professional man to make his home in. Harry moved into 29 Crosthwaite Park West, a large terraced house overlooking a small railed-in park, and because of Mrs. Synge's desire to be close to her family, No. 31 next door, a corner house, was also acquired. Soon a door was broken between the two gardens and through it the Stephens children, Francis, Edward and Claire, were always coming and going. They came to catch mice for their grandmother, to do her accounts or plant lettuce in the garden while she, saddened that her son John was a non-believer, did her best to inculcate religion into them in return.

The young Stephens were fascinated by their uncle, particularly Edward, and many a night unknown to his mother or grandmother he would creep back through the garden to sit in the parlour with him. As they sat talking, the fire and its flickering would illuminate Synge's collection of birds' eggs assembled on the bureau and the starling he had stuffed which lay immobile under a glass case. These evenings became part of the memories Edward incorporated in his book, *My Uncle John.*

144

Now that the family lived close to the sea, Mrs. Synge decided to change the venue for their summer holidays and began renting houses in the mountains of County Wicklow, a part of the country which since the mid-eighteenth century had been associated with the Synges. The connection went back to 1765 when one John Hatch, who owned large estates in Wicklow, Dublin and Meath, married a Synge. The Synges were a distinguished Protestant family which came from England in the seventeenth century; originally they bore the name Millington but, according to family tradition, this was changed to Synge when a far distant ancestor pleased some English monarch by his sweet singing voice. John Hatch, who lived at Roundwood Park near the village of Roundwood, produced only two daughters but most conveniently both married their first cousins, the sons of their mother's brother Edward Synge of Syngefield, Birr, County Offaly. One of them, Francis, the writer's great-grandfather built up the Hatch estates in County Wicklow until at one time his lands stretched ten miles from the heights of Djouce Mountain to Carrick Hill. He also acquired a new seat for the family, Glenmouth, overlooking the Devil's Glen at Ashford, a noted beauty spot, which he enlarged, building towers at each of its corners and renaming it Glanmore Castle. Though it was dismantled many years later, the house which has since been rebuilt and stands at the end of a long avenue looks much the same as it did when John was brought there as a child to visit his uncle Francis and aunt Editha. In those days visitors would be met at the railway station in Rathnew and taken the last few miles to Glanmore in a four-in-hand. It remained in the family until 1943.

The house which the Synges now rented regularly in the summer was Castle Kevin, a square stone house, now painted white, on high ground outside the village of Annamoe, not far from Glanmore. The home of the Frizelle family, it was named after the original thirteenth-century castle where Red Hugh O'Donnell, the great Irish chieftain from Donegal, was said to have sheltered after his escape from captivity in Dublin Castle. While the Synges were there, it was under boycott. The Land League had been founded in 1879 to protect the rights of tenant farmers, and the following year Charles Stewart Parnell, himself a Protestant and a landowner but also leader of the Irish Parliamentary Party, introduced the strategy of 'boycotting' or ostracizing any landlord who was considered unjust. Old Aunt Jane Synge, sister of John's father, used to recall how Parnell, as the child of neighbours, had been dandled on her lap at Glanmore, and she would say with regret that she wished she had choked him in infancy.

The boycott did not affect the Synge family's holidays, though occasionally two policemen would wander up the long avenue to check everything was all right. John spent his time fishing for trout in the Annamoe river, going for picnics with the family and roaming the countryside, taking notes from the local people, both of the stories they told him and their manner of speech. Best of all must have been the summer of 1894 when Cherrie Matheson came to stay. She was a friend of his cousin Florence Ross and he had first met her at Greystones where her family also holidayed, the friendship later continuing because she lived at No. 25 Crosthwaite Park. Already Synge, who called her his *Scherma,* was in love with her. At Castle Kevin he spoke to her of Wordsworth and Corot and played for her on his violin. Once they watched the sun go down, from a cairn near the house. He was to propose marriage to her some time later but she refused him, for she was a member of the Plymouth Brethren and would not consider marrying someone with his unorthodox views. It was an experience that affected him deeply.

The garden at Castle Kevin was a most romantic if overgrown place, where raspberry canes and thistles grew together in a tangled mass and where the apple trees were covered in lichen and moss. Thinking perhaps of the Synge estate, Glanmore, which had dwindled in size and in style over the years, this garden became to John a symbol of a world that was dying: 'In this garden one seemed to feel the tragedy of

*Tomriland House
(left) – the porch and
top windows have
been altered since
Synge's time
Tiglin farmhouse
(right)*

the landlord class also, and of the innumerable old families that are
quickly dwindling away. These owners of the land are not much pitied
at the present day or much deserving of pity; and yet one cannot quite
forget that they are the descendants of what was at one time, in the
eighteenth century, a high-spirited and highly cultivated aristocracy.'

When not at Castle Kevin, the Synges stayed at other houses in the
locality, like Avonmore House, and Casino, a dower house on the
estate of Avondale, ancestral home of Charles Stewart Parnell. They
were frequent visitors to Tiglin farmhouse, now a youth hostel, where
his aunt Editha lived when Glanmore was rented, and to Uplands.
This house, at the top of a steep avenue on the main road between
Annamoe and Roundwood, had been built by old aunt Emily who,
with some understatement, called it her cottage.

John also stayed at Tomriland House at Tomrilands Cross, and
there he wrote much of the plays *In the Shadow of the Glen* and *Riders to
the Sea*, typing away on a table in his bedroom which was over the
kitchen. As a study he also had the glass-sided porch in the front of the
house where geraniums grew in abundance. Here he lived in closer
proximity to the servants than at the larger Castle Kevin and he
benefitted from listening to their dialogue:'When I was writing *In the
Shadow of the Glen* I got more aid than any learning could have given me,
from a chink in the floor of the old Wicklow house where I was staying,
that let me hear what was being said by the servant girls in the
kitchen.'

Synge left Trinity with an undistinguished degree but he had been
awarded a scholarship in counterpoint by the Royal Academy of

148

Music and later went to Germany to study music. However, by 1894 he had given up the idea of making music his career and with thoughts of becoming a teacher went to Paris, a city he was to visit almost every winter for a number of years.

The year 1896 was a turning point in his life. Cherrie Matheson finally refused him and in December he met Yeats at the Hotel Corneille in Paris. He had by then written a few poems and was jotting down his impressions in essays. When he left Paris the following May he carried with him Yeats's famous advice: 'Go to the Aran Islands. Live there as if you were one of the people themselves; express a life that has never found expression.'

The three Aran islands are eight miles off the coast of County Galway, and the life there, Synge felt, was perhaps the most primitive left in Europe. He was not the first Synge to visit Aran; his uncle Alexander had spent several years there as a Protestant missionary. The writer himself was to spend four and a half months on the islands, in several visits. At first he stayed in the Atlantic Hotel on Inishmore, the biggest of the islands, and although he also visited Inisheer, where he stayed at Michael Costello's public house, most of his time was spent on the middle island, Inishmaan, where he lodged with the family of Pat MacDonagh. The house was also the post-office, and on an island with no priest, doctor or policeman resident, it was the focal point for the islanders. John had a room just beside the hub of the cottage, the kitchen. Here he learned Irish from the son of the house, Martin, listened to the stories of the island *seanachi* Pat Dirane, ate eggs and mackerel, and rocked the cradle when there was a baby in the house.

He occasionally played his fiddle for the family but most of his time was spent out of doors, tramping up to Dun Conor in his pampooties or taking photographs of the islanders with his shiny mahogany Lancaster camera. He recorded such unique sights as the harvesting of the seaweed for kelp and the cattle being swum out to the steamer at the beginning of each summer on their way to be fattened in Connemara on the grass of which the island itself was short. He saw the sea bring death to many a house and heard the terrible keen sent up over every dead body. In this cry of pain he felt the inner consciousness of the people laid itself bare for an instant: 'They are usually silent, but in the presence of death all outward show of indifference or patience is forgotten, and they shriek with pitiable despair before the horror of the fate to which they all are doomed.' He loved Aran and was always lonely when he was leaving: 'The sort of yearning I feel towards those lonely rocks is indescribably acute.'

In later years both Padraic Pearse and Thomas MacDonagh, two signatories of the Irish proclamation of independence who were to be executed, also stayed at Pat MacDonagh's cottage on Inishmaan.

After his first visit to Aran, Synge was invited to Coole Park and from then on was gradually drawn into the Irish literary circle. He was writing all the time and though his book *The Aran Islands* was first rejected by two publishers, and Lady Gregory rejected one of his plays for the newly formed Irish Literary Theatre, he persevered.

Synge's holidays were now spent mostly in the south of Ireland, in County Kerry. He sometimes stayed at Mountain Stage near Glenbeigh in the cottage of Philly Harris who told him stories of Oisín, Tír na nÓg and the Fenian heroes, and about the Celtic Vahalla which was reputed to lie across the bay on the Dingle peninsula. Another time he went to the Longs at Ballyferriter and visited the Blasket Islands where he stayed with Padraig O Cathain. His last Kerry visit was to Thady Kavane's cottage in Ventry. He also visited Mayo and Sligo, and, with his brother, took a fishing holiday in Donegal, staying at Milford. In 1905 *The Manchester Guardian* commissioned Synge and Jack B. Yeats to write a series of articles on the poverty-stricken areas of the west of Ireland.

In December 1904 the Irish Literary Theatre became the Abbey, and the following year saw the first performance of *The Well of the Saints*. As Synge's involvement with the Abbey grew he needed to live

closer to town, so he left Crosthwaite Park to live in various flats, and had short stays at 15 Maxwell Road, Rathmines, and at 57 Rathgar Road. Meanwhile the Stephens had moved to Silchester House, a large house in its own grounds beside the church, on the corner of Silchester Road in Glenageary, and Mrs. Synge was lucky enough to find a small house nearby with the grandiose name of Glendalough House. John often stayed with her and it was here that he finalized *The Playboy of the Western World*. After breakfast, dressed in an old jacket and waistcoat, his cycling knickerbockers and knitted stockings, he would sit working in his bedroom, breaking off at lunchtime to walk up Adelaide Road to the garden gate of Silchester House of which he had a key so that he could come and go as he pleased. After lunch there, he would sit in the garden relaxing.

Molly Allgood, the sister of Sara, joined the Abbey Theatre in 1905 and she and Synge fell in love; he loved her, he once said, more than any woman had been loved in Ireland for a thousand years. He found a flat at 47 York Road, Rathmines, for 13/6d a week, and there they planned to live. This was to be the only real home of his own Synge ever had. Eagerly he furnished it with all the miscellaneous bits and pieces he could get – a bed lent by a cousin, a sugan chair brought from Kerry, a print of a Giorgione painting. Together, in the bow-windowed drawing-room, he and Mollie sat planning the life together which they would never have. They also visited Wicklow, Synge staying at Mrs. McGuirk's cottage in Glencree, Molly and Sara nearby.

He was at this stage very ill. Hodgkin's disease had first manifested itself in 1897 and there had been a number of operations. When, after a

*Silchester House (far left)*
*Glendalough House (left)*
*47 York Road (right)*

period home on leave, his brother Samuel was returning to his work as a medical missionary in China something told him he might never see John again: 'We said goodbye and then he stood on the pier as the steamer started, and something seemed to say to me within, "He won't be here when you come back."'

In 1908 he had to have a further operation, later convalescing with the Stephens before going back to Glendalough House. His mother was also ill and perhaps because he could not face her death he went to Germany where he continued working on *Deirdre of the Sorrows*. Mrs. Synge died in October of that year.

In January 1909 he was back in hospital again, at the Elphis Nursing Home, now the Convent of the Sisters of Marie Auxiliatrice at 19 Lower Mount Street. He sipped a few drops of champagne a day or two before he died and in a room filled with March sunlight listened by the open window, straining to hear over the song of the thrush, the note of the first blackbird. In a farewell letter to Molly he wrote: 'My dearest love, this is a mere line for you, my poor child, in case anything goes wrong with me tomorrow, to bid you good-bye and ask you to be brave and good, and not to forget the good times we've had, and the beautiful times we've seen together.'

He died on 24 March 1909, a few weeks before his thirty-eighth birthday, and is buried in the family plot in Mount Jerome cemetery, Dublin.

# Oscar Wilde

## 1854-1900

---

Genius has often been born of the union of two totally disparate people, and this was certainly true of Oscar Fingal O'Flahertie Wilde, born in Dublin in October 1854.

His father was William Wilde, a distinguished eye and ear specialist who was appointed Surgeon-Oculist to Queen Victoria when he was not yet forty years of age; he was a Connaught man whose father had been a doctor in Castlereagh in County Roscommon and whose mother was one of the Fynnes of Ballymagibbon near Cong in County Mayo. Oscar's mother, born Jane Francesca Elgee, was the daughter of a County Wexford solicitor and a grand-niece of the novelist, Charles Robert Maturin, who, after her father died, lived with her widowed mother at 34 Lower Leeson Street in Dublin. She was also a nationalist and at the funeral of the patriot Thomas Davis was so moved that she became a supporter of the Young Ireland movement and wrote enthusiastically for its paper, *The Nation,* under the pen names of John Fenshaw Ellis and Speranza. When she married William Wilde it was a union between two brilliant and highly individualistic people and from the start their home, at 21 Westland Row, became a meeting place for intellectuals. It was in this moderately sized Georgian house, the back windows of which look out over Trinity College Park, that the couple's second son, Oscar, was born.

Soon afterwards, the Wildes moved to 1 Merrion Square, a few hundred yards away. Merrion, one of Dublin's famous Georgian squares, was a most prestigious address; here the most eminent doctors practised, living alongside the doyens of the legal profession, one or two peers, a few judges and various members of parliament.

*21 Westland Row (left)*
*Esplanade Terrace, Bray (right)*

The Wilde's house, designed by John Ensor, on a corner, had both balconies and a sun-room and was among the most imposing in the Square.

Speranza's salon was thronged by the notable Dubliners of her day, among them the writers Sir Samuel Ferguson, Sheridan Le Fanu and Charles Lever; William Rowan Hamilton, the mathematician; George Petrie, the archaeologist; and Isaac Butt, the lawyer. So large were the gatherings that sometimes guests had to be content to crowd into the downstairs rooms, though it was upstairs on the first floor, in the drawing-room overlooking the square, that the lady of the house held court. She had an aversion to harsh light so she received no one before five in the evening and even then, though it was often still daylight, insisted on the shutters being drawn so that her soirées took place by the light of only a few shaded oil lamps. Dressed in voluminous crinolines, white powder on her face and weighed down with jewellery, she orchestrated the conversation, occasionally summoning her sons, Willie and Oscar, to be shown off to the company. Oscar's memories of his youth were heavily laced with celebrities, from William Smith O'Brien who had been imprisoned in Tasmania for his part in the abortive rising of 1848, to John Mitchel who, for his part in the same event, had been sent to Van Dieman's Land in Northern Australia. Meeting him later at the dinner table in Merrion Square, Oscar was impressed in particular by his eagle eye and impassioned manner.

William became Sir William in 1864 and the social success of the Wilde family seemed assured. But the same year saw him involved in a particularly lurid scandal. He had had liaisons with various women

156

and eventually one of these, a patient of his called Mary Josephine Travers, determined to cause trouble. She maintained that he had interfered with her while she was attending him, and through word of mouth and published pamphlet she made sure that her allegations became widely known. Some years previously William Wilde had built four houses, numbers 1 to 4 Esplanade Terrace, in the seaside resort of Bray, County Wicklow, twelve miles south of Dublin, and when his wife took the children out there to avoid the unpleasantness caused by the scandal, Miss Travers sent out small boys to pester them by flaunting copies of the pamphlet. Eventually the matter came to court and though Mary Travers only received damages of a farthing, Sir William was a broken man.

Two years after the trial, another traumatic blow befell the family. Isola, their third child, died at the age of nine while on a visit to Sir William's sister, Emily, and her husband, the Reverend Mr. Noble, at the Glebe House, Edgeworthstown, County Longford. Speranza had always yearned for a daughter, a yearning expressed by dressing Oscar in girl's clothes, and when Isola did arrive she became the darling of the whole family. After her death, the twelve-year-old Oscar visited her grave in the village cemetery day after day. When he died, an envelope containing a lock of her hair, decorated outside with wreaths, crosses and biblical quotations was found in his possession. Written on the front, in large childish letters, were the words, 'My Isola's hair'.

Sir William had to endure an additional family tragedy. Two of his illegitimate children, Emily and Mary Wilde, lived with his brother Ralph, in County Monaghan. While attending a ball at Drumaconner

*Moytura,*
*Lough Corrib ( left )*
*Earlscliff, Howth*
*( right )*

House on the road between Smithboro and Monaghan, the muslin crinoline of one of the sisters caught fire and when the other sister tried to help to put out the flames she too was engulfed. Though both girls were rushed out of the house and rolled in the snow by their hosts they were too badly burned to survive. They are buried in the cemetery at Drumsnatt, County Monaghan.

By this time Oscar had joined his brother Willie at Portora Royal School, Enniskillen, County Fermanagh. Oscar, unlike his brother, didn't mix well with the other boys and spent much time out rowing by himself on Lough Erne. By his own account he spent too much time at Portora reading English novels and poetry and generally dreaming the years away. At the age of sixteen he discovered the Greek classics.

After the trial, Sir William spent much of his time in the west of Ireland, and Willie and Oscar frequently spent holidays at either one of the two homes he had there. One, Illaunroe Lodge, was situated in one of the remotest parts of Connemara, between Leenane and Tully Cross in County Galway, not far from the spectacular inland fiord of Killary Bay. At the Lodge, which jutted out into Lough Fee, the boys would go shooting and they fished not only in the lake that surrounded the house but in nearby Lough Muck and the river Calfin. The second house was in County Mayo where Sir William had acquired a farm of 170 acres when the estate of his mother's family, the Fynnes, was sold. There he built Moytura, a two-storey house with front porch and eaved roof looking out over Lough Corrib and across through its islands to the town of Oughterard. As a neighbour the Wildes had Lord

Ardilaun, a member of the Guinness brewing family, then busily occupied in transforming his father's French chateau into the Gothic Ashford Castle. Sir William, who was also an archaeologist of renown, wrote about this area around Cong in his book, *Lough Corrib and Lough Mask*.

At the age of seventeen Oscar won a scholarship to Trinity College in Dublin. With his brother he lived on the quadrangle named Botany Bay by the students after the infamous convict colony of the same name in Australia. There on the first floor of Number 18 they shared rooms consisting of two bedrooms, a sitting-room and a pantry larder. At Trinity, Oscar came under the influence of one of the most brilliant scholars of his time, John Pentland Mahaffy, Professor of Ancient History. Even when he went to Oxford, his friendship with Mahaffy was maintained by expeditions together to Italy and Greece. In the summer of 1876 he spent much of his time at his old professor's home, Earlscliff in Howth, writing to a friend: 'I am here with that dear Mahaffy every day. He has a charming house by the sea here, on a place called the Hill of Howth (one of the crescent horns that shuts in the Bay of Dublin), the only place near town with fields of yellow gorse, and stretches of wild myrtle, red heather and ferns.'

However, when Oscar was later tried in London and sentenced to two years' hard labour for homosexual practices, Mahaffy is said to have commented, on hearing his name, 'We no longer speak of Mr. Oscar Wilde.' Mahaffy later became Provost of Trinity.

But this was all in the future. Oscar had a brilliant career at Trinity, winning a Foundation Scholarship in classics and the Berkeley Gold

Medal for Greek. He finished by winning a scholarship to Magdalen College, Oxford, which he entered in October 1874.

Sir William died when Oscar was in his second year at Oxford. Moytura and Merrion Square were left to Willie; Oscar got the houses in Bray and he shared Illaunroe with one of his father's illegitimate children, Dr. Henry Wilson. Most of the property, however, was heavily mortgaged and soon they sold both Merrion Square and the Bray houses, on which Oscar made something less than £3,000. He had by now decided to become 'a poet, a writer, a dramatist' and obviously London was a better spring-board than Dublin. Willie was also there, working as a journalist, and soon Speranza followed her sons to England.

Oscar did, however, continue to visit the west of Ireland for some time. From there he wrote to a friend: 'I am sure you will like this wild mountainous country, close to the Atlantic and teeming with sport of all kinds. It is in every way magnificent and makes me years younger than actual history records . . . . My fishing lodge is situated on Lough Fee near Leenane and the Killary Bay, and three miles from the sea; it is a small two-storied cottage furnished in bachelor fashion for three persons but would accommodate more.' Eventually both Illaunroe and Moytura were sold.

Though much of his youth was spent in England, it was in Ireland that Oscar fell in love for the first time. The young lady was Florence Balcombe, daughter of a retired army officer who lived at No. 1 Marino Crescent in the north city suburb of Clontarf. She later married Bram Stoker, author of *Dracula,* who also lived on the Crescent, at No. 15. Oscar later recalled the time of his romance with Florence as the two sweetest years of his youth. When she announced her engagement to Stoker he wrote and asked her to return a gold cross he had given her one Christmas morning long before, writing: 'Though you have not thought it worthwhile to let me know of your marriage, still I cannot leave Ireland without sending you my wishes that you may be happy; whatever happens I at least cannot be indifferent to your welfare; the currents of our lives flowed too long beside one another for that.'

Later he met and fell in love with Constance Lloyd, daughter of a prominent QC, Horace Lloyd; he died when she was young and her mother married again. Though Constance lived in London, it was at

*Illaunroe Lodge, Connemara. The house is one-storey in front, two-storey at the back*

the home of her maternal grandmother Mrs. Atkinson, at 1 Ely Place. Dublin, that Oscar proposed to her. They were married in London in 1884.

Constance was the mother of his sons Cyril and Vyvyan but after the trial of 1895 he never saw them again. Nevertheless it was Constance who came to Reading gaol to break the news to him of his mother's death, at the beginning of 1896, travelling from Italy to do so. When, after his release, he heard that she was dangerously ill he wrote to a friend: 'I am simply broken-hearted by what you tell me. I don't mind my life being wrecked – that is as it should be – but when I think of poor Constance I simply want to kill myself.' She died in April 1898 and when he visited her grave in Genoa he was filled with a sense of the uselessness of all regrets: 'Nothing could have been otherwise and life is a very terrible thing.'

Wilde died not long afterwards, on 30 November 1900, at the Hotel d'Alsace in Paris. He was buried at Bagneux cemetery but some years later his body was moved to Père Lachaise, 89th division, where it rests underneath an Epstein sculpture. Carved on his tomb is the epitaph:

> *And alien tears will fill for him*
> *Pity's long broken urn.*
> *For his mourners will be outcast men*
> *And outcasts will always mourn*

# William Butler Yeats

## 1865-1939

Though William Butler Yeats was born in a suburban house in Dublin, at 5 Sandymount Avenue, the territory of his childhood was, without a doubt, County Sligo. Emphasizing how much this western seaboard county meant to him he later wrote of it: 'I have walked on Sindbad's yellow shore and never shall another's hit my fancy.'

Though his great-grandfather, John Yeats, had introduced a Sligo connection into the family in the early nineteenth century by becoming rector to the parish of Drumcliff, it was through his mother's family that the poet really came to know the county. Born Susan Pollexfen she came from an old-established family of ship owners and millers, none of whom were too pleased when her young husband, John Butler Yeats, gave up his career as a barrister to try and make a living as a painter in London. Certainly the change was hard on Susan who, as often as she could, took her children home to Ireland for holidays on board one of her father's ships, either *The Sligo* or *The Liverpool*. Later Yeats was to write: 'In a sense Sligo has always been my home.'

There was always room for the Yeats children at Merville, the grey stone eighteenth-century home of their grandparents, William and Elizabeth Pollexfen, which was set in grounds of sixty acres and had in those days fourteen bedrooms. Today it is a part of the Nazareth home for old people and children.

For a child Merville was a treasure house, filled from top to bottom with exciting things collected by their grandfather in his seafaring days. There were the Chinese pictures on rice paper, the ivory walking stick from India, the coral collection and, above all, the jar of water from the Jordan with which Pollexfen offspring were baptized. The

*5 Sandymount Avenue (above) and Merville, Sligo*

children had a room with four windows, two of which looked out over the stable yard and two over the gardens. Then out beyond the immediate environs of the house was the larger landscape of Sligo with the hill of Knocknarea on one side and the majestic peak of Ben Bulben across the estuary on the other. Here they breakfasted at 9 am and dined at 4 pm and it was considered self-indulgent to eat anything between meals.

At Merville Willie had two dogs to play with, a red pony to ride, and trips to take in the family carriage, sitting up beside Scanlan the coachman. Though Willie spent some time at school he was also free to browse in the so-called library which only contained some old novels and an encyclopaedia, and to listen to the stories that the servants had to tell him. It was while staying there that a friend explained to him 'all the mechanism of sex', an experience he later remembered as the first breaking of the dream of childhood.

Still the house was rather a stern place to grow up in, dominated as it was by the personality of grandfather Pollexfen, larger than life to such a degree that as a child Willie confused him with God. An austere type of man, one abiding memory the poet had of him was how, even as an old man, he slept with a hatchet by his bedside in case of an intrusion by burglars. Aware that his eldest son was emotional, sensitive and intellectual, John Butler Yeats worried about his being so long there, and later the poet did record that he had had an unhappy childhood, caused partly, if inadvertently, by his grandfather: 'Some of my misery was loneliness and some of it fear of old William Pollexfen, my grandfather. He was never unkind, and I cannot remember that he ever spoke harshly to me, but it was the custom to fear and admire him.'

The people of Sligo had the same admiration for him and honoured him with roadside bonfires when he was returning from a journey. A measure of the position he held in the town can be gauged from the fact that when Willie's little brother, Robert, died as a child, the ships in Sligo harbour lowered their flags to half-mast as a mark of sympathy.

In London Willie was acutely lonely for Sligo: 'I longed for a sod of earth from some field I knew, something of Sligo to hold in my hand.' He later wrote of his love for the county which was kept alive by their mother: 'She would spend hours listening to stories or telling stories of the pilots and fishing people of Rosses Point, or of her own Sligo

*Charlemont House,*
*Sligo*

girlhood, and it was assumed between her and us that Sligo was more beautiful than other places .'

When an aunt in Sligo told him once that while in Sligo he was somebody but in London nobody, she was probably referring not only to the family's position in the county but to the fact that he had so many relatives there and was associated with so many houses. When they left Merville, his grandparents moved to Charlemont House, high up on a hill overlooking the Garavogue River, just outside the town, before the turn off to Rosses Point. Later they went to Rathedmond on the other side of town, on the road to Strandhill, with a view across the water to Ben Bulben.

Then there were the two homes of his great-uncle William Middleton to visit. The first of these was Avena House in Ballysadare where the Pollexfen and Middleton mills were situated, their wheels driven by the gushing waters of the Owenmore river. Here Willie listened to endless stories told by the gardener Paddy Flynn and played with his cousins around the salmon weir, waterfall and rapids. In summertime he would visit them at their seaside home Elsinore, right by the water's edge in Rosses Point; a house that had a special charm for the children because it was said once to have been a smugglers' haunt. Some dead smuggler, the children believed, came back occasionally to give, as his signal, three loud raps on the drawing-room window at sundown. 'One night I heard them very distinctly,' Willie later wrote. From Elsinore the children would row in the river mouth or occasionally be taken sailing in a heavy slow schooner yacht or in a big ship's boat that had been ribbed and decked. Sadly this house, which has a view of the

*Rathedmonde (left above)*
*Avena House, Ballysadare*
*(left centre)*
*Fort Louis, Rathbraughan*
*(left below)*
*Seaview, Cregg (right)*

Metal Man buoy made famous by the poet's painter brother Jack in his painting *Memory Harbour*, has now fallen into ruin.

There were also some Yeatses left in the vicinity. The poet's great-aunt Mary Yeats, called great-aunt Micky, lived in the townland of Cregg, on a hill looking over at Knocknarea across the channel that separates Rosses Point from Sligo. Her farmhouse, Seaview, is, like all these houses, still standing today, though without the creeper that grew on it in Willie's day. It was here, he wrote in *Reveries over Childhood and Youth*, that he saw for the first time the crimson streak of the gladiolus and awaited with excitement, its blossom.

Great-aunt Micky was full of family history. She had a cream jug with the Yeatses' motto and crest upon it, and also a silver cup with the Butler crest and a piece of paper inside that gave all its history for generations, until unfortunately some caller used it to light up his pipe.

At Rathbraughan, in a long one-storey building on the banks of the Rathbraughan river, lived the poet's great-uncle, Matthew Yeats, who had a big family of boys and girls with whom Willie used to sail toy boats on the river outside. His house was called Fort Louis, and the name of some member of the Yeats family can still be seen scratched into the fireplace in an upstairs bedroom.

When in Sligo in later years, Willie would stay with his uncle George Pollexfen at his house Thornhill, the first of a pair of semi-detached houses on the road from Sligo to Strandhill, almost opposite Rathedmond. He also stayed at uncle George's house, Moyle Lodge in Rosses Point.

The Pollexfens were of a morose disposition, with more than one of

167

them suffering from mental illness; but the other side of Willie's family too had its unhappy members, one of whom was Robert Corbet, an uncle of John Butler Yeats. It was in the grounds of his mock-Gothic Sandymount Castle, which though somewhat changed is still standing today, that Willie was wheeled in his pram as a little boy, taking fright according to his nurse at the deer that roamed through the grounds. There was in those days a lake in the parkland frequented by ducks and swans, while on an island in the middle two eagles were chained to a post. Later however Uncle Robert killed himself and so, when the Yeats family returned to Ireland in 1880, it was not to Sandymount they came but to the seaside village of Howth on the north side of Dublin.

Here their first home was a then-thatched house on the cliffs called Balscadden where Willie removed the glass from his bedroom window to allow the seaspray to come in and soak him at night. Later they moved to Island View, a house just on Howth harbour, but Willie, still a lover of the open air, often slept out at night sometimes among the rhododendrons in the demesne of Howth Castle, sometimes in a niche up on the cliffs, a candle, cocoa and some biscuits with him for provisions. Each morning he travelled into Dublin with his father who had a studio at 44 York Street, a street which in the early nineteenth century had associations with writers James Clarence Mangan and Charles Robert Maturin, but which has since sadly been almost totally demolished. There painter father and his son would eat breakfast together, John Butler furthering Willie's education by reciting for him the great speeches from *Coriolanus* and other works. Later John Butler

*Moyle Lodge, Rosses Point (far left)*
*Thornhill, Sligo (left)*
*– the house is on the left*
*10 Ashfield Terrace, now*
*418 Harold's Cross Road (right)*

Yeats had a studio at 7 St. Stephen's Green.

Aware that his son must have some formal schooling he had him enrolled at The High School, then in Harcourt Street. Later he became a student at the College of Art in Kildare Street where he met George Russell (AE). By then the family was living in the city again, this time at 10 Ashfield Terrace, now known as 418 Harold's Cross Road. Here, when all the family had gone to bed, Willie and George Russell would cook themselves a meal in the kitchen and stay up half the night chanting their verses at one another.

Through his life Yeats was to divide his time between Ireland and London, and it was there in 1889 that he met Maud Gonne or, as he later put it, that the troubling of his life began. He had heard in letters from home of this beautiful girl who had left the society of the Viceregal Court for Irish nationalism and when he met her he fell in love. Though that love was never requited, it proved to be the shaping force of his life. Among other things the meeting defined clearly for him his love of Ireland and he returned there often, especially to Sligo.

Now a writer and outside the confines of any social class he was free to visit the big houses that had been outside his ken as a child. Explaining it he wrote: 'In my childhood I had seen on clear days from the hill above my grandmother's house or from the carriage if our drive was towards Ben Bulben or from the smooth grass hill of Rosses the grey stone walls of Lissadell among its trees. We were merchant people of the town. No matter how rich we grew, no matter how many thousands a year our mills or our ships brought in, we could never be "county" nor indeed had we any desire to be so. We would meet on

169

Grand Jurys those people in the great houses – Lissadell among its woods, Hazelwood House by the lake's edge and Markree Castle encircled by wood after wood – and we would speak no malicious gossip and know ourselves respected in turn but the long settled habit of Irish life set up a wall.' Now as a young man he was free to spend time with the people who lived in such houses, particularly the Gore-Booth girls of Lissadell, Eva, whom he likened to a gazelle, and Constance, 'acknowledged beauty of the county', who was later, as Countess Markiewicz, to be prominent in the 1916 Rising. Lissadell, built of Ballysadare limestone, was a classical house with, he wrote, 'a great sitting-room as high as a church and all things in good taste'. Today open to the public, its rooms filled with period furniture and fine china, the house echoes with the words Yeats wrote of it.

It was at this time too that Yeats really began to explore the countryside around Sligo town, particularly Lough Gill where his favourite spot was the tiny heathery island of Innisfree, not far from the shore at the end of the lake, under Killery Mountain. Those who are familiar with his poems know that he also immortalized in his work the rock of Dooney on Lough Gill which in his day was a meeting-place for outdoor country dances on Sunday evenings, the music being supplied by James Howley, a blind fiddler from Ballysadare.

Writing to the poet Katharine Tynan from Sligo he defined his feel- ings for the county: 'The very feel of the familiar Sligo earth puts me in good spirits. I should like to live here always, not so much out of liking for the people as for the earth and the sky here, though I like the people too.' Another time he told her that Sligo was to him the loneliest place in the world: 'Going for a walk is a continual meeting with ghosts. For Sligo for me has no flesh and blood attractions – only memories and sentimentalities accumulated here as a child, making it more dear than any other place.' In later life, however, Sligo was to some extent replaced by Lady Gregory's home at Coole Park, outside Gort in County Galway.

When in Dublin, he had many short term addresses including 53 Mountjoy Square, the Nassau Hotel in South Frederick Street and a boarding-house in St. Lawrence's Road in Clontarf called Lonsdale House. After his marriage in 1917 to Miss George Hyde-Lees he did, however, have a number of more permanent homes in Ireland. Chief among these was Thoor Ballylee, the mediaeval tower set amid ancient

*Lough Gill, Sligo (above), and Lissadell*

*Ben Bulben, Sligo (left)*
*Thoor Ballylee,*
*near Gort (right)*

ash trees by the River Cloon not far from Gort, which he bought from the Congested Districts Board for £35. Enthusiastically he set about restoring it, getting in the local mason and blacksmith and the carpenter to make sturdy furniture for it in oak and in elm! 'I am making a setting for my old age,' he wrote at the time. Though the Civil War raged through the country during his early years there, the poet and his wife were content; he writing in his study, she planting flowers and vegetables in abundance on the acre of land outside.

To his friend in America, John Quinn, he wrote: 'Out of door with the hawthorn all in blossom all along the river banks, everything is so beautiful that to go elsewhere is to leave beauty behind.' Happily the Tower is still preserved in his memory, leaving as yet unfulfilled the words he had inscribed there in his lifetime.

> *I, the poet William Yeats,*
> *With old millboards and sea-green slates,*
> *And smith work from the Gort forge,*
> *Restored this tower for my wife George;*
> *And may these characters remain*
> *When all is ruin once again*

Because of both its dampness and its isolated setting The Tower was not lived in full time by the Yeatses who had two children. They also had homes in Dublin, the first being at 73 St. Stephen's Green which Maud Gonne, the owner, let them have for a low rent. Later they bought 82 Merrion Square, a Georgian house in one of the most

*82 Merrion Square (far left)*
*42 Fitzwilliam Square (left)*
*Riversdale (right)*

prestigious parts of the city and close to Leinster House where for a time Yeats sat as a member of the Irish Senate. Later they lived briefly in a rented house in Howth, Brook Lawn, before taking the top-floor flat at 42 Fitzwilliam Square which with her usual vigour George spent much time decorating. To Lady Gregory he wrote that his wife had made the place charming, providing for him a study that looked out over the square, with blue walls and ceiling and golden-coloured curtains. This flat was succeeded by a brief sojourn at a house on Killiney Hill.

Yeats's last home in Ireland was in Rathfarnham. With apple and cherry trees, herbaceous border, bowling-green, croquet and tennis lawns, Riversdale and its grounds was the perfect setting for a poet and after some initial reservations he came to love it: 'At first I was unhappy, for everything made me remember the great trees of Coole, my home for nearly forty years, but now that the pictures are up I feel more content. This little creeper-covered farm-house might be in a Calvert woodcut, and what could be more suitable for one's last decade.' With lilies on the pond and roses of all descriptions in its borders, it was hardly surprising that the garden had some fame among gardeners, so much so that once, when Yeats planned a trip to London in the spring, the gardener persuaded him to postpone it, saying that he couldn't miss the garden in the month of April.

Here he could beat his family at croquet, live in his old age on milk, peaches and grapes from his own garden and wander at will from his study into the fruit garden 'to share the gooseberries with the bull finches'. Here, in his study adorned with a Burne-Jones window and

pictures by his father, his brother Jack, and Lady Gregory's dead son Robert, he wrote many of his last poems and planned for his burial. He died in the south of France at Cap Martin in 1939.

Interred initially at Roquebrune, nine years later his body was brought home abroad the Irish corvette *Macha* on a voyage that took altogether eleven days. As it was feared that the channel at Sligo might be too narrow for the vessel it sailed instead into Galway Bay where the coffin was met by Yeats's widow and his brother Jack before being piped ashore. Then came the poet's last journey, by road from Galway to Sligo where a military guard of honour was waiting. Appropriately the Government was represented by Sean MacBride, Minister for External Affairs, but also the son of Maud Gonne. And so at Drumcliff in the graveyard of the church where his great-grandfather had been Rector, Yeats was buried, his own epitaph on his tombstone:

> *Cast a cold eye*
> *On life, on death.*
> *Horseman, pass by!*

# Acknowledgments

*The Homes of Irish Writers* contains many quotations. As far as possible the source of these extracts has been traced and the copyright-owners' permission obtained. Any omission is inadvertent and will be rectified in a future edition.

The author and publishers would like to thank the following publishers and agents for permission to quote copyright material.

## INTRODUCTION

Batsford, London (*My Ireland* by Kate O'Brien).

Chapman & Hall, London (*The Wild Irish Girl: The Life of Sydney Owenson, Lady Morgan* by Lionel Stevenson).

The Educational Co. of Ireland, incorporating Longman Browne & Nolan (*Three Homes* by Lennox and Tom Robinson and Nora Dorman).

Goldsmith Press, The Curragh (*Patrick Kavanagh Country* by Dr. Peter Kavanagh).

Heinemann, London (*Presentation Parlour* by Kate O'Brien).

## AE (GEORGE RUSSELL)

Abelard-Schuman, London (*Letters from AE*)

Curtis Brown, London, on behalf of John Child-Villiers and Valentine Lamb as literary executors of Lord Dunsany (*My Ireland* by Lord Dunsany).

Macmillan, London and Basingstoke (*A Memoir of AE* by John Eglinton).

Smith Elder, London (*Twenty Five Years. Reminiscences* by Katharine Tynan).

Colin Smythe, Gerrards Cross, Bucks (*That Myriad-Minded Man* by Henry Summerfield).

## ELIZABETH BOWEN

Curtis Brown, London, Literary executors of the Estate of Elizabeth Bowen (*Seven Winters* by Elizabeth Bowen).

Virago Press, London (*Bowen's Court* by Elizabeth Bowen).

## WILLIAM CARLETON

Talbot Press, Dublin (*Carleton's Country* by Rose Shaw).

### LORD DUNSANY

Curtis Brown, London, on behalf of Mark Heathcoat Amory (*Lord Dunsany* by Mark Amory); also on behalf of John Child-Villiers and Valentine Lamb as literary executors of Lord Dunsany (*My Ireland* and *Patches of Sunlight* by Lord Dunsany).

### MARIE EDGEWORTH

Faber & Faber, London (*The Black Book of Edgeworthstown and other Edgeworth Memories,* edited by Harriet Jessie Butler and Harold Edgeworth Butler).

### OLIVER ST. JOHN GOGARTY

Sphere Books, London, and by permission of Oliver D. Gogarty (*As I Was Going Down Sackville Street, It Isn't This Time of Year at All, Rolling Down the Lea,* and *Tumbling in the Hay,* all by Oliver St. John Gogarty).

### LADY GREGORY

Macmillan, London and Basingstoke ( *Inishfallen Fare Thee Well* by Sean O'Casey).

Putnam, London (*Journals 1916 – 1930* by Lady Gregory, edited by Lennox Robinson).

Colin Smythe, Gerrards Cross, on behalf of the Lady Gregory Estate (*Coole* by Lady Gregory, and *Me and Nu. Childhood at Coole* by Anne Gregory).

A.P. Watt, London, on behalf of Michael and Anne Yeats (*Autobiographies* by W. B. Yeats).

### JAMES JOYCE

Faber & Faber, London, and Viking Penguin Inc. New York (*The Letters of James Joyce, Vol. 1,* edited by Stuart Gilbert, copyright 1957, 1966 by The Viking Press; *The Letters of James Joyce, Vol. 2,* edited by Richard Ellmann, copyright 1966 by F. Lionel Munro, as Administrator of the Estate of James Joyce).

### FRANCIS LEDWIDGE

Constable, London (*The Years of the Shadow* by Katharine Tynan).

Curtis Brown, London, on behalf of John Child-Villiers and Valentine Lamb as literary executors of Lord Dunsany (*My Ireland* by Lord Dunsany).

Dr. Andrew Rynne (*Francis Ledwidge; A Life of the Poet* by Alice Curtayne).

John Shanahan (*Letter to Lizzie Healy*).

### CHARLES LEVER

Chapman & Hall, London (*Dr. Quicksilver. The Life of Charles Lever* by Lionel Stevenson, and *The Irish Sketchbook* by M. A. Titmarsh).

### GEORGE MOORE

Gollancz, London (*The Life of George Moore* by Joseph Hone).

Colin Smythe, Gerrards Cross (*Hail and Farewell* by George Moore).

Jonathan Cape, London (*The Moores of Moore Hall* by Joseph Hone).

### SEAN O'CASEY

Macmillan, London and Basingstoke (*Autobiography* by Sean O'Casey, and *Sean* by Eileen O'Casey).

### GEORGE BERNARD SHAW
Allen Figgis, Dublin (*Crowned Harp* by Nora Robertson).
A. P. Watt, London (*Bernard Shaw* by Hesketh Pearson).

### SOMERVILLE AND ROSS
Faber & Faber, London (*Somerville and Ross* by Maurice Collins).
John Farquharson, London (*Irish Memories* and *Wheeltracks*).

### JOHN MILLINGTON SYNGE
Belknap Press of Harvard University Press, Mass. (*Letters to Molly* by J. M. Synge).
Oxford University Press (*My Uncle John: Edward Stephens's Life of J. M. Synge*, edited by Andrew Carpenter; and *The Aran Islands* by J. M. Synge, 1907).
Talbot Press, Dublin (*Letters to my Daughter* by the Rev. Samuel Synge).

### OSCAR WILDE
Hart-Davis (*Letters of Oscar Wilde*, edited by Rupert Hart-Davis, 1962).
Oxford University Press (*Selected Letters of Oscar Wilde*, edited by Rupert Hart-Davis, 1979).
Routledge & Kegan Paul, London (*Mahaffy* by W. B. Stanford and R. B. McDowell).

### WILLIAM BUTLER YEATS
A. P. Watt, London, on behalf of Michael and Anne Yeats (*Autobiographies* and *Memoirs* by W. B. Yeats; *The Letters of W. B. Yeats*, edited by Allan Wade).

*Elsinore, Rosses Point*

# *Bibliography*

## INTRODUCTION

GENERAL

Cronin, Anthony, *Dead as Doornails. A Memoir*. Dolmen Press, Dublin, 1976.

Eagle, Dorothy, and Carnell, Hilary (editors), *The Oxford Literary Guide to the British Isles*. Clarendon Press, Oxford, 1977.

Flanagan, Thomas, *The Irish Novelists 1800–1850*. Columbia University Press, New York, 1959.

Kenny, Herbert A., *Literary Dublin*. Gill & Macmillan, Dublin, 1974.

WILLIAM ALLINGHAM

Allingham, William, *A Diary*. Macmillan, London, 1907.

Warner, Alan, *William Allingham*. Bucknell University Press, USA, 1975.

DION BOUCICAULT

Walsh, Townsend, *The Career of Dion Boucicault*. Dunlap Society, New York, 1915.

PADRAIC COLUM

Bowen, Zack, *Padraic Colum. A Biographical–Critical Introduction*. Southern Illinois University Press, USA, 1970.

AUBREY DE VERE

Ward, Wilfrid, *Aubrey de Vere*. A Memoir based on his unpublished diaries and correspondence. Longmans Green, London, 1904.

SIR SAMUEL FERGUSON

Ferguson, Lady Mary Catherine, *Sir Samuel Ferguson in the Ireland of his Day*, 2 vols. Blackwood, Edinburgh and London, 1896.

McCahan, Robert, *The Life of Sir Samuel Ferguson;* Northern Constitution, Coleraine.

GEORGE FITZMAURICE

Slaughter, Howard K., *George Fitzmaurice and his Enchanted Land*. The Irish Theatre series, Dolmen Press, 1972.

OLIVER GOLDSMITH

Sells, A. Lytton, *Oliver Goldsmith – His Life and Works*. George Allen & Unwin, London, 1974.

GERALD GRIFFIN

Gill, W. S., *Gerald Griffin, Poet, Novelist, Christian Brother*. Gill, Dublin, 1940.

– Griffin, *The Life of Gerald Griffin*, by his brother. James Duffy, Dublin 1857.

Mannin, Ethel, *Two Studies in Integrity. Gerald Griffin and The Rev. Francis Mahony (Father Prout)*. Jarrolds, London, 1954.

PATRICK KAVANAGH

Kavanagh, Peter, *Patrick Kavanagh. Sacred Keeper, A Biography*. Goldsmith Press, The Curragh, County Kildare, 1980.

LADY MORGAN

Morgan, Lady, *The Book of the Boudoir*. Henry Colburn, London, 1829.

Stevenson, Lionel, *The Wild Irish Girl; the Life of Sydney Owenson, Lady Morgan*. Chapman & Hall, London. 1936.

KATE O'BRIEN

O'Brien, Kate, *Presentation Parlour*. Heinemann, London, 1963.

– *My Ireland*. Batsford, London, 1962.

LENNOX ROBINSON

Robinson, Lennox, Robinson, Tom, and Dorman, Nora, *Three Homes*. Browne & Nolan, Dublin, 1938.

RICHARD B. SHERIDAN

Fitzgerald, Percy, *The Lives of the Sheridans*, Vols. 1 and 2. Bentley, London, 1886.

JAMES STEPHENS

Pyle, Hilary, *James Stephens. His work and an account of his life*. Routledge & Kegan Paul, London, 1965.

BRAM STOKER

Ludlam, Harry, *A Biography of Bram Stoker*. New English Library, 1977.

KATHARINE TYNAN

Rose, Marilyn Gaddis, *Katharine Tynan*. Bucknell University Press, USA, 1974.

AE (GEORGE RUSSELL)

AE, *Letters from AE*, edited by Alan Denson. Abelard-Schuman, London, 1961

– *The Living Torch*, edited and introduced by Monk Gibbon. Macmillan, London, 1937.

Eglinton, John, *A Memoir of AE*. Macmillan, London, 1937.

Summerfield, Henry, *That Myriad-Minded Man. A biography of George William Russell*. Colin Smythe, Gerrards Cross, Bucks, 1975.

Tynan, Katharine, *Twenty Five Years. Reminiscences*. Smith Elder, London, 1913.

JOHN AND MICHAEL BANIM

Murray, Patrick Joseph, *The Life of John Banim*. Sadlier, New York, 1857.

ELIZABETH BOWEN

Bowen, Elizabeth, *Bowen's Court*. Longmans Green, London 1942. Virago Press. (paperback), London.

– *Pictures and Conversations*, Allen Lane, London, 1975.

– *Seven Winters*. Longmans Green, London, 1943.

Gill, Richard, *Happy Rural Seat. The English Country House and the Literary Imagination*. Yale University Press, New Haven, 1972.

Glendinning, Victoria, *Elizabeth Bowen*. Weidenfeld & Nicolson, London, 1977.

WILLIAM CARLETON

Carleton, William, *The Autobiography of William Carleton,* with preface by Patrick

Kavanagh. MacGibbon & Kee, London, 1968.

Kiely, Ben, *Poor Scholar. A study of the works and days of William Carleton*. Talbot Press, Dublin, 1972.

O'Donoghue, D. J., *The Life of William Carleton*. Downey, London, 1896.


LORD DUNSANY

Amory, Mark, *Lord Dunsany: A Biography*. Collins, London, 1972.

Curtayne, Alice, *Francis Ledwidge*. Martin Brian and O'Keefe, London, 1972.

Dunsany, Lord, *My Ireland*. Jarrolds, London, 1937 (reprinted 1950).

– *Patches of Sunlight*. Heinemann, London, 1938.


MARIA EDGEWORTH

Butler, Harriet Jessie and Butler, Harold Edgeworth (editors), *The Black Book of Edgeworthstown*. Faber & Gwyer, London, 1927.

Butler, Marilyn , *Maria Edgeworth, A Literary Biography*. Clarendon Press, Oxford, 1972.

Edgeworth, Frances, *A Memoir of Maria Edgeworth*. Joseph Masters, London, 1867.

Edgeworth, Richard Lovell, *Memoirs of Richard Lovell Edgeworth* (begun by him and concluded by his daughter), 2 vols. Hunter, London, 1820.

Hare, Augustus J. C., *Life and Letters of Maria Edgeworth*. Edward Arnold, London, 1894.


OLIVER ST. J. GOGARTY

Gogarty, Oliver St. John, *As I Was Going Down Sackville Street,* Rich & Cowan, London, 1937. Sphere Books (paperback), London.

– *It Isn't This Time of Year at All; an unpremeditated autobiography*. MacGibbon & Kee, London, 1954. Sphere Books (paperback), London.

– *Rolling Down the Lea*. Constable, London, 1950. Sphere Books (paperback), London.

– *Tumbling in the Hay,* Constable, London, 1939. Sphere Books (paperback), London.

Lyons, J. B., *Oliver St. John Gogarty*. Bucknell University Press, USA, 1976.

O'Connor, Ulick, *Oliver St. John Gogarty. A Poet and his Times*. Jonathan Cape, London, 1964.


LADY GREGORY

Adams, Hazard, *Lady Gregory*. Bucknell University Press, USA, 1973.

Coxhead, Elizabeth, *Lady Gregory: a Literary Portrait*. Secker & Warburg, London, 1966.

Gregory, Anne, *Me and Nu. Childhood at Coole*. Colin Smythe, Gerrards Cross, 1978.

Gregory, Lady Augusta, *Coole*. The Cuala Press, Dublin, 1931.

– *Journals 1916–1930* (editor Lennox Robinson). Putnam , London, 1946.

– *Journals,* Volume 1. Colin Smythe, Gerrards Cross, 1978.

Mikhail, E. H., (editor), *Lady Gregory. Interview and Recollections*. Macmillan, London, 1977.

O'Casey, Sean, *Inishfallen, Fare Thee Well*. Macmillan, London, 1949.

Smythe, Colin, *A Guide to Coole Park*. Van Duren Press, Bucks., 1973.

Yeats, W. B., *Dramatis Personae 1896–1902*. Macmillan, London, 1936.


JAMES JOYCE

Ellmann, Richard, *James Joyce,* Oxford University Press (paperback), 1965.

Joyce, James, *The Letters of James Joyce*, Vol. 1, edited by Stuart Gilbert. Faber & Faber, London, 1957.

– *The Letters of James Joyce*, Vols. 2 and 3, edited by Richard Ellmann. Faber & Faber, London, 1966.

Joyce, Stanislaus, *My Brother's Keeper*. Faber & Faber, London, 1958.

### FRANCIS LEDWIDGE

Curtayne, Alice, *Francis Ledwidge*. Martin Brian & O'Keefe, London, 1972.

Dunsany, Lord, *Introductions to Ledwidge's 'Songs of Peace' and 'Songs of the Field'*. Jenkins, London. 1916.

– *My Ireland*. Jarrolds, London, 1937.

Tynan, Katharine, *The Years of the Shadow*. Constable, London, 1919.

### CHARLES LEVER

Fitzpatrick, W. J., *The Life of Charles Lever*. Downey, London, 1896.

Stevenson, Lionel, *Dr. Quicksilver: The Life of Charles Lever*. Chapman & Hall, London, 1939.

Titmarsh, M. A., *The Irish Sketchbook*. Chapman & Hall, London, 1843.

### GEORGE MOORE

Hone, Joseph, *The Life of George Moore*. Gollancz, London, 1936.

– *The Moores of Moore Hall*. Jonathan Cape, London, 1939.

Moore, George, *Hail and Farewell*, 3 Vols., *Ave, Salve, Vale*. William Heinemann, London, 1937.

### SEAN O'CASEY

Krause, David, *Sean O'Casey; the Man and his Work*. Macmillan, New York, 1960.

O'Casey, Eileen, *Sean*, Macmillan, London, 1971.

O'Casey, Sean, *Autobiography*, 6 vols., Macmillan, London, 1949.

### GEORGE BERNARD SHAW

Pearson, Hesketh, *Bernard Shaw*. Macdonald & Jane's, London, 1975.

Shaw, G. B., *The Collected Letters of George Bernard Shaw, 1874-1910*, 2 vols., edited by Dan H. Lawrence, Max Reinhardt, London, 1965.

Shenfield, Margaret, *Bernard Shaw. A Pictorial Biography*. Thames & Hudson, London, 1962.

### SOMERVILLE AND ROSS

Collis, Maurice, *Somerville and Ross, A Biography*. Faber & Faber, London, 1968.

Cummins, Geraldine, *Dr. E. OE. Somerville. A Biography*. Andrew Dakers, London, 1952.

Powell, Violet, *The Irish Cousins; the Books and the Background of Somerville and Ross*. Heinemann, London, 1970.

Somerville and Ross, *Irish Memories*. Longmans Green, London, 1917.

– *Wheeltracks*. Longmans, London, 1923.

### JOHN MILLINGTON SYNGE

Greene, David H., and Stephens, Edward M., *J. M. Synge 1871–1909*. Macmillan, New York, 1959.

Synge, J. M., *Autobiography*, edited by Alan Price. Dolmen Press, Dublin, 1965.
– *Collected Works*, Vol. 1., edited by Robin Skelton; Vol. 2, edited by Alan Price; Vols. 3 and 4, edited by Ann Saddlemyer. Oxford University Press, 1961–8.
– *In Wicklow , West Kerry and Connemara*. O'Brien Press, Dublin, 1980.
– *Letters to Molly*, edited by Ann Saddlemyer. The Belknap Press of Harvard University Press, Cambridge, Mass., 1971.
– *The Aran Islands*. Oxford University Press (paperback), 1979.
Stephens, Edward (edited by Andrew Carpenter), *My Uncle John*. Oxford University Press, London, 1974.

OSCAR WILDE
Wilde, Oscar, *Letters of Oscar Wilde*, edited by Rupert Hart-Davis. Hart-Davis, London, 1962.
– *Selected Letters of Oscar Wilde*, edited by Rupert Hart-Davis. Oxford University Press, London, 1979.
Holland, Vyvyan, *Oscar Wilde. A Pictorial Biography*. Thames & Hudson, London, 1960.
Montgomery Hyde, H., *Oscar Wilde*. Magnum Books, Metheun Paperbacks, London, 1977.
Pearson, Hesketh, *The Life of Oscar Wilde*. Metheun, London, 1946.
Stanford, W. B., and McDowell, R. B., *Mahaffy*. Routledge & Kegan Paul, London, 1971.

WILLIAM BUTLER YEATS
Hanley, Mary, *Thoor Ballylee, home of William Butler Yeats*. Dolmen Press, Dublin, 1965
Hone, Joseph, *W. B. Yeats*. Macmillan, London, 1967.
Jeffares, A. Norman, *W. B. Yeats. Man and Poet*. Routledge & Kegan Paul, London, 1949.
Kirby, Sheelah, *The Yeats Country*, Dolmen Press, Dublin, 1962.
McGarry, James, *Place Names in the Writings of William Butler Yeats*. Colin Smythe, Gerrards Cross, 1976.
MacLiammoir, Michael, and Boland, Eavan, *W. B. Yeats and his World*. Thames & Hudson, London, 1971.
Murphy, William M., *Prodigal Father. The Life of John Butler Yeats*. Cornell, USA, 1978.
Tuohy, Frank, *Yeats*. Macmillan, London, 1976.
Yeats, W. B., *Autobiographies*. Macmillan, London, 1955.
–*Letters of W. B. Yeats*, edited by Allan Wade. Rupert Hart-Davis. London, 1954.
– *Memoirs*, Macmillan, London, 1972.

# Illustrations

The numbers are those of the pages on which the illustrations appear. Photographs from the Lawrence Collection by courtesy of the National Library of Ireland.

# *Index*

As a general rule, houses and places associated with writers in the introduction are not indexed unless there is an illustration; for reference, look under individual authors. Figures in italics indicate illustrations.

*The mills, seen from Avena House, Ballysadare*